A Deleuzian Critique of Queer Thought

Plateaus – New Directions in Deleuze Studies

'It's not a matter of bringing all sorts of things together under a single concept but rather of relating each concept to variables that explain its mutations.'
Gilles Deleuze, *Negotiations*

Series Editors
Ian Buchanan, University of Wollongong
Claire Colebrook, Penn State University

Editorial Advisory Board
Keith Ansell Pearson, Ronald Bogue, Constantin V. Boundas, Rosi Braidotti, Eugene Holland, Gregg Lambert, Dorothea Olkowski, Paul Patton, Daniel Smith, James Williams

Titles available in the series
Christian Kerslake, *Immanence and the Vertigo of Philosophy: From Kant to Deleuze*
Jean-Clet Martin, *Variations: The Philosophy of Gilles Deleuze*, translated by Constantin V. Boundas and Susan Dyrkton
Simone Bignall, *Postcolonial Agency: Critique and Constructivism*
Miguel de Beistegui, *Immanence – Deleuze and Philosophy*
Jean-Jacques Lecercle, *Badiou and Deleuze Read Literature*
Ronald Bogue, *Deleuzian Fabulation and the Scars of History*
Sean Bowden, *The Priority of Events: Deleuze's Logic of Sense*
Craig Lundy, *History and Becoming: Deleuze's Philosophy of Creativity*
Aidan Tynan, *Deleuze's Literary Clinic: Criticism and the Politics of Symptoms*
Thomas Nail, *Returning to Revolution: Deleuze, Guattari and Zapatismo*
François Zourabichvili, *Deleuze: A Philosophy of the Event* with *The Vocabulary of Deleuze* edited by Gregg Lambert and Daniel W. Smith, translated by Kieran Aarons
Frida Beckman, *Between Desire and Pleasure: A Deleuzian Theory of Sexuality*
Nadine Boljkovac, *Untimely Affects: Gilles Deleuze and an Ethics of Cinema*
Daniela Voss, *Conditions of Thought: Deleuze and Transcendental Ideas*
Daniel Barber, *Deleuze and the Naming of God: Post-Secularism and the Future of Immanence*
F. LeRon Shults, *Iconoclastic Theology: Gilles Deleuze and the Secretion of Atheism*
Janae Sholtz, *The Invention of a People: Heidegger and Deleuze on Art and the Political*
Marco Altamirano, *Time, Technology and Environment: An Essay on the Philosophy of Nature*
Sean McQueen, *Deleuze and Baudrillard: From Cyberpunk to Biopunk*
Ridvan Askin, *Narrative and Becoming*
Marc Rölli, *Gilles Deleuze's Transcendental Empiricism: From Tradition to Difference*, translated by Peter Hertz-Ohmes
Guillaume Collett, *The Psychoanalysis of Sense: Deleuze and the Lacanian School*
Ryan J. Johnson, *The Deleuze-Lucretius Encounter*
Allan James Thomas, *Deleuze, Cinema and the Thought of the World*
Cheri Lynne Carr, *Deleuze's Kantian Ethos: Critique as a Way of Life*
Alex Tissandier, *Affirming Divergence: Deleuze's Reading of Leibniz*
Barbara Glowczewski, *Indigenising Anthropology with Guattari and Deleuze*
Koichiro Kokubun, *The Principles of Deleuzian Philosophy*, translated by Wren Nishina
Felice Cimatti, *Unbecoming Human: Philosophy of Animality After Deleuze*, translated by Fabio Gironi
Ryan J. Johnson, *Deleuze, A Stoic*
Jane Newland, *Deleuze in Children's Literature*
D. J. S. Cross, *Deleuze and the Problem of Affect*
Laurent de Sutter, *Deleuze's Philosophy of Law*, translated by Nils F. Schott
Andrew M. Jampol-Petzinger, *Deleuze, Kierkegaard and the Ethics of Selfhood*
Nir Kedem, *A Deleuzian Critique of Queer Thought: Overcoming Sexuality*
Timothy Deane-Freeman, *Deleuze, Digital Media and Thought*

Forthcoming volumes
Justin Litaker, *Deleuze and Guattari's Political Economy*
Sean Bowden, *Expression, Action and Agency in Deleuze: Willing Events*
Axel Cherniavsky, *Deleuze and the Creation of Concepts: Philosophy and Methodology*, translated by Taylor Adkins

Visit the Plateaus website at edinburghuniversitypress.com/series/plat

A DELEUZIAN CRITIQUE OF QUEER THOUGHT

Overcoming Sexuality

Nir Kedem

EDINBURGH
University Press

Edinburgh University Press is one of the leading university presses in the UK. We publish academic books and journals in our selected subject areas across the humanities and social sciences, combining cutting-edge scholarship with high editorial and production values to produce academic works of lasting importance. For more information visit our website: edinburghuniversitypress.com

© Nir Kedem, 2024, 2025

Edinburgh University Press Ltd
13 Infirmary Street,
 Edinburgh, EH1 1LT

First published in hardback by Edinburgh University Press 2024

Typeset in 11/13 Sabon LT Std by
by Cheshire Typesetting Ltd, Cuddington, Cheshire

A CIP record for this book is available from the British Library

ISBN 978 1 4744 4157 5 (hardback)
ISBN 978 1 4744 4158 2 (paperback)
ISBN 978 1 4774 4159 9 (webready PDF)
ISBN 978 1 4744 4160 5 (epub)

The right of Nir Kedem to be identified as the author of this work has been asserted in accordance with the Copyright, Designs and Patents Act 1988, and the Copyright and Related Rights Regulations 2003 (SI No. 2498).

For Sarel

Contents

Acknowledgements	viii
Abbreviations	x
Introduction: We Are No Longer Queer...	1
Overcoming Sexuality	1
What is a Deleuzian Critique?	7
Nous autres, Queers	17
1 Queer Theory's Image of Thought	21
Mis-introductions	26
A Theory to Come	33
Critique, Abstractions and Universals	37
2 Philosophically Queer: Constructing a Concept	48
Conceptual Personae: The Exemplary Saint	60
The Double-Faced Concept	70
Thought and Freedom	79
What Can a Concept Do?	95
3 Pozitive Bodies of Resistance	108
Relays of Theory and Practice	108
The Missing Body	110
The Poz: A Joyful Body, without Pleasure or Desire	117
ACT UP	124
New Queer Cinema	130
Conclusion: The Virality to Come, the Virality that Is	145
Bibliography	148
Index	155

Acknowledgements

This book could not have been published without the support and love of so many people I feel fortunate to have had in my life. Ian Buchanan has been a mentor and friend whose conviction in me and in this project has been relentless and uncompromising, even and particularly when life threatened to suck me into its many upheavals. I am forever grateful for all of these and for never letting me lose sight of what matters and why it matters. Orly Lubin – whom my own mother sees as my second mother – has been the vibrant force that shaped and guided my thinking and work in feminist theories and queer theories (and cinema studies and literary theory), and that has ceaselessly pushed me towards becoming the critical scholar I have been aspiring to be. Over the years she has generously bestowed on me her love, care, friendship, wisdom, humour, and wit, not to mention countless days and nights in New York of talking shop, culture, and life. Hannan Hever open-handedly conferred on me the invaluable knowledge and tools so vital for becoming a skillful writer and a professional. He lovingly yet meticulously oversaw my compiling of the book proposal and made sure I felt free to ask for his advice on any issue. Together, Orly and Hannan opened their hearts to me as well as their home, and made sure I'd always feel at home.

Special thanks to Carol Macdonald at EUP, whose professionalism is surpassed only by her warmth and unsparing thoughtfulness, for unfailingly being there to guide and reassure me every step of the way, doing above and beyond to make a novice author like me feel that I'm in the best of hands. I could not have hoped for a finer editor to guide me through this arduous journey.

Special thanks to the unwitting Deleuzian Michal Schoenberg-Taz for constantly labouring to set me up for success, making sure that I'd nourish my soul and body, and helping me with love and compassion to find my bearings whenever I was lost.

Acknowledgements

Finally, I'm deeply thankful for the unconditional love and care I'm fortunate to have received from my parents and from my family, both by blood and choice: Liad Solomon, Udi Hochberg, Yoad Bar Noy, Yoram Elkaim, and Tomer Shechner. And last but not least, thank you to Dana, my son Hillel, and my partner Sarel.

Abbreviations

Works by Gilles Deleuze

AO *Anti-Oedipus*, with Felix Guattari, trans. Robert Hurley, Mark Seem and Helen R. Lane, Minneapolis: University of Minnesota Press, 1983

B *Bergsonism*, trans. Hugh Tomlinson and Barbara Habberjam, New York: Zone Books, 1991

D *Dialogues II*, with Claire Parnet, trans. Hugh Tomlinson, Barbara Habberjam and Eliot Ross Albert, New York: Columbia University Press, 2002

DI *Desert Islands and Other Texts 1953–1974*, trans. Michael Taormina, ed. David Lapoujade, New York: Semiotext(e), 2004

DR *Difference and Repetition*, trans. Paul Patton, New York: Columbia University Press, 1994

F *Foucault*, trans. Seán Hand, Minneapolis: University of Minnesota Press, 1988

LOT *Letters and Other Texts*, ed. David Lapoujade, trans. Ames Hodges, New York: Semiotext(e), 2020

N *Negotiations 1972–1990*, trans. Martin Joughin, New York: Columbia University Press, 1995

NP *Nietzsche & Philosophy*, trans. Hugh Tomlinson, New York: Columbia University Press, 1983

SPP *Spinoza: Practical Philosophy*, trans. Robert Hurley, San Francisco: City Lights, 1988

TI *Cinema 2: The Time-Image*, trans. Hugh Tomlinson and Barbara Habberjam, Minneapolis: University of Minnesota Press, 1989

TP *A Thousand Plateaus*, trans. Brian Massumi, Minneapolis: University of Minnesota Press, 1987

Abbreviations

TRM   *Two Regimes of Madness: Texts and Interviews 1975–1995*, trans. Ames Hodges and Mike Taormina, New York: Semiotext(e), 2007

WP   *What is Philosophy?*, with Félix Guattari, trans. Hugh Tomlinson and Graham Burchell, New York: Columbia University Press, 1994

Works by Michel Foucault

AK   *Archeology of Knowledge*, trans. A. M. Sheridan Smith, New York: Routledge, 2002

BBP   *The Birth of Biopolitics: Lectures at the Collège de France 1978–1979*, trans. Graham Burchell, ed. Michel Senellart, New York: Palgrave, 2008

E   *Ethics*, trans. Robert Hurley et al., ed. Paul Rabinow, New York: New Press, 1997

FL   *Foucault Live: Collected Interviews, 1961–1984*, trans. Lysa Hochroth and John Johnston, ed. Sylvère Lotringer, New York: Semiotext(e), 1989

GS   'The Gay Science', trans. Nicholae Morar and Daniel W. Smith, *Critical Inquiry* 37 (2011): 385–403

GSO   *The Government of Self and Others: Lectures at the Collège de France 1982–1983*, trans. Graham Burchell, ed. Frédéric Gros, New York: Palgrave, 2010

HS   *The Hermeneutics of the Subject: Lectures at the Collège de France 1981–1982*, trans. Graham Burchell, ed. Frédéric Gros, New York: Palgrave, 2005

HV1   *The History of Sexuality, Volume 1: The Will to Knowledge*, trans. Robert Hurley, New York: Pantheon, 1978

PK   *Power/Knowledge: Selected Interviews and Other Writings 1972–1977*, trans. Colin Gordon et al., New York: Pantheon, 1980

POT   *The Politics of Truth*, ed. Sylvère Lotringer, Los Angeles: Semiotext(e), 1997

POW   *Power*, trans. Robert Hurley et al., ed. James D. Faubion, New York: New York University Press, 2000

SAP   'The Subject and Power', in H. L. Dreyfus and P. Rabinow (eds), *Michel Foucault: Beyond Structuralism and*

Abbreviations

Hermeneutics, 2nd edn, Chicago: University of Chicago Press, 1983, 208–26

Works by David M. Halperin

HTB *How to be Gay*, Cambridge, MA: Belknap Press of Harvard University Press, 2012
HTD *How to Do the History of Sexuality*, Chicago: University of Chicago Press, 2002
NOR 'The Normalization of Queer Theory', *Journal of Homosexuality*, 45(2–4) (2003): 339–43
SF *Saint Foucault: Towards a Gay Hagiography*, New York: Oxford University Press, 1995

Introduction: We Are No Longer Queer ...

Overcoming Sexuality

In an interview from 1978, Foucault seems to have set what remains today the greatest challenge to queer theory: 'you not only have to liberate your sexuality ... we also have to liberate ourselves even from this notion of sexuality' (GS 388). Influenced by Foucault's work on sexuality, the AIDS crisis and the dominance of the gender paradigm in American feminist theories, queer theory emerged as an interdisciplinary research field in the early 1990s in the United States, holding the promise of radical new ways to transform political thought and activism. Although it reclaimed 'queer', an otherwise derogatory word for homosexuals, as a positive term, instated it as a malleable, transformative, conceptual tool for thinking political resistance, and developed compelling critiques of dominant conceptions of sexuality, queer theory to date has nevertheless demonstrated a deep commitment to the very notion of sexuality. This may seem obvious and a non-issue, but in this book it is precisely the status of sexuality as a privileged term and a precious tenet in queer theory that undergoes a thorough problematisation.

While the last two decades have seen a growing body of scholarship that ardently enlists Deleuze's philosophical toolbox to expand (and celebrate) queer theory's ideas of sexuality (along with sex, desire and pleasure), here I employ Deleuze's philosophy to posit sexuality as a problem – an impediment even, dare I say – for queer theory; or, more precisely, for queer theory's proclaimed potential to revolutionise our ways of thinking and acting. I do not therefore share the zeal with which some pronounce Deleuze's work ultimately or always-already queer, or that 'the erotic *is* Deleuzian' (Stark 2017: 58), or that 'everything is potentially sexualised through Deleuze's philosophy' (Beckman 2011: 3). In fact, I argue the opposite: sexuality has no privileged status in Deleuze's philosophy. In a correspondence with Arnaud Villani dated 20 October 1980, when asked about the relationship between sexuality and his work,

Deleuze's answer was unequivocal: 'It would be true up to *Logic of Sense*, where there is still an expressible relationship between sexuality and metaphysics. After that, sexuality appears to me as more of a poorly established abstraction' (LOT 77).

Deleuze's response applies to much of his work, including his collaborations with Guattari and others. Let us take *Anti-Oedipus* as an example. To argue that the two volumes of *Capitalism and Schizophrenia* 'may be seen as a two-step project toward the freeing of sexuality' rather than the freeing of ourselves from sexuality, that *Anti-Oedipus* 'is in one sense all about sex, which reflects the main message of the book', and that their concept of desire 'is explicitly explored in its relation to sexuality' (Beckman 2011: 8) is reductive and untenable. I have already discussed elsewhere the very non-sexual function of sex and sexuality in *Anti-Oedipus*, which I will not reiterate here.[1] My primary concern at this point is rather to assert the slender interest Deleuze and Guattari have in sexuality as we know it. In an interview with Raymond Bellour, Guattari says

> The term sexuality is fucked up. There is no more important flux on the level of sexuality . . . the word sexuality itself is already an entrance, an avenue towards the oedipalization of desiring energy . . . Desiring energy does not know sexes, it doesn't know persons, it doesn't even know objects. (LOT 209)

Deleuze then confirms this, saying that they do not hold any specialised sense of sexuality: 'whatever you like sexually, what you are investing through it, whether it is a woman, a man, a piece of clothing, a shoe, a chicken, whatever, it is a social political field' (LOT 210). Sexuality and sexual difference are not important privileged terms for them; rather, against psychoanalysis's view of sexuality as undergoing sublimation in the social field, Deleuze insists that 'There is only a sexuality that is the same throughout and inundates everything . . . it invests the social field directly. It is social, political' (LOT 211), as are fantasies and delirium – 'All delirium possesses a world-historical, political, and racial content' (AO 88), just as 'fantasy is never individual: it is *group fantasy*' (AO 30). When Deleuze says that delirium 'is the fundamental state of sexuality' (LOT 217), it is precisely because the libido is not sublimated; rather, it directly invests the social field rather than some psychic reality that is supposedly separate from the social one, as psychoanalysis wants us to believe (AO 30).

Introduction

Several years later, Deleuze's stand against privileging sexuality has not changed:

> We do not believe in general that sexuality has the role of an infrastructure in the assemblages of desire, nor that it constitutes an energy capable of transformation or of neutralization and sublimation. Sexuality can only be thought of as one flux among others ... No assemblage can be characterized by one flux exclusively ... The more it is articulated with other fluxes, the more it will remain sexuality, pure and simple sexuality, far from all idealizing sublimation. (D 101–2)

So against views about Deleuze's so-called inherently queer and sexual philosophy, and against the unquestioned assumption that queer theory is and has always been about sexuality, this book advocates an argument for the overcoming of sexuality, underpinned by Deleuze's philosophy and its sober, dispassionate outlook on sexuality.[2] Before I expand on what I mean by this, let us first return to the problematisation of sexuality. Chapter 1 discusses why and how sexuality has become an impediment for queer theory, but first I elaborate the quote from Foucault about our needing to liberate ourselves from sexuality.

There is nothing natural, universal or innocent about sexuality, Foucault argued in the first volume of *The History of Sexuality*. His analysis showed that sexuality (and homosexuality) as we conceive it today is rather a historically modern Western notion, which emerged mainly in the nineteenth century in multiple discourses and institutions, and which is inseparable from a rather new formation of power that had begun to emerge already in the eighteenth century. In *History*, Foucault defined power as a dynamic, strategic situation consisting in a network of agonistic relations that traverse (and continually transform) the entire social field. In a later interview shortly before his death, Foucault explained succinctly that 'Power is relations; power is not a thing, it is a relationship between two individuals ... such that one can direct the behaviour of another or determine [it]' (FL 410). Here he introduces the term 'government' as a broader, reworked concept of power: 'When I say "govern someone", it simply means in the sense that one can determine one's behaviour in terms of a strategy by resorting to a number of tactics' (FL 410). Sexuality, therefore, is but the nomenclature of a grouping together of select strategies – what Foucault termed a *dispositif* – designed to both discipline individual bodies and regulate the behaviour of populations.[3] Such a *dispositif* conforms to specific interests and goals of the historical (yet impersonal) formation of power called biopower. Put simply, what we call 'sexuality', assuming it to be a natural (and sometimes pathological) trait that applies universally, and the key to our discovering the truth about ourselves, is an intricate device of social control; a device used to regulate, direct, alter or prevent our behaviours, according to the needs and ends of power. When one declares 'I'm gay' or 'I'm a lesbian' or even 'I'm queer', one believes oneself to be freely and positively asserting one's own identity for oneself and others alike. The successful struggles of the gay liberation movements in the late 1960s and queer AIDS activism in the 1980s and 1990s undeniably played a fundamental part in making this possible. They fought to liberate our sexuality from the reins of power that had long been persecuting, proscribing, shaping and normalising it. Yet at the same time, and despite its many successes, this so-called liberation has been tying us (and our sexuality) ever more tightly to power's grip. Why? Because by taking it upon ourselves to discover who we truly are by endlessly speaking the truth of our sexuality to ourselves and others alike, we are making ourselves easy targets for power – we adopt the very *dispositif* of sexuality (along with the definitions, traits, behaviours and whatnot) imposed on us by power, even if we do this by way of resistance (as did the sexual liberation movements). We turn ourselves into easily identifiable objects of control, because embracing our sexuality makes us visible to power.

Strangely, queer theory has been unwittingly complicit with the preserving and reinforcing of the *dispositif* of sexuality, long before any attempt to ally itself with Deleuze. Against the better judgement of many of its founding figures, queer theory has established itself as a theory *of* sexuality, which has been losing sight of its foundational concept's – that is, queer's – in principle indeterminacy; its conceptual power to dismantle the notion of sexuality and thus to revolutionise queer thought and activism's potential ways to fight oppression and injustice. The more queer theory attaches itself to sexuality, the more it dwindles and restricts its own potential to be used as a critical tool for resistance.

Overcoming sexuality is thus what guides my Deleuzian inquiry into queer theory, its limits and potential for transformation. Functioning as both political vision and ideal end, the overcoming of sexuality marks radically new possibilities for queer thought and new futures for queer theory, activism and art. It regards sexuality not as its cause or end, but rather as its point of departure – a gateway

Introduction

to an unknown that lies beyond the sexualised present; one that enables imagining and thinking new, desexualised modes of existence that could (and did, as discussed in Chapter 3) engender new forms of resistance to power and its ever-renewing and rapidly adaptive strategies of control. Foucault's envisioning a new role for the sexual liberation movements coincides with the sense of overcoming sexuality explained above, and it might as well have described the road not taken by queer theory. These movements, he said,

> must be understood as movements of affirmation 'beginning with' sexuality... [they] take off from sexuality, from the apparatus of sexuality within which we're trapped, which make it function to the limit; but at the same time, those movements are displaced in relation to sexuality, disengaging themselves from it and going beyond it. (FL 217)

Foucault does not go into much detail about how to overcome sexuality or what desexualised modes of existence look like. He occasionally and usually briefly referred to various examples, but refrained from suggesting prescriptions. His 'going beyond sexuality' begins by substituting the concept of pleasure for that of desire. Desire for Foucault is a discursive tool used to code and explicate pleasure as sexual pleasure, which enables biopower to define standards of normal (and abnormal) sexuality, and thus to effectively normalise both individuals and whole populations. These processes of normalisation make one a subject, in both senses of the word – one is individuated and subjugated at one and the same time, by the same means (GS 389). Pleasure, on the other hand, is 'an event that is not assigned, and is not assignable, to a subject' (GS 390). It is rather a means to 'desubjugate yourself, [to] cease being a subject, an identity. It is like an affirmation of nonidentity' (GS 399–400), by which one becomes different from oneself, or by which one experiences a temporary shattering of the self. So long as the concept of desire is used to conflate pleasure with sex, we will keep looking for (and finding) the 'truth' about ourselves in our sexuality, 'whereas we should be striving, rather, toward a desexualization, to a general economy of pleasure that would not be sexually normed' (FL 212).

Desexualisation in Foucault's sense is discussed in detail in Chapter 2, but I employ it here somewhat differently (though still related to Foucault's sense). Obviously, Deleuze scholars were not the first to attempt to 'sexualise' everything by employing Deleuze's philosophy; it is what queer theory has been doing all along. Its attachment to sexuality leads precisely to the sexualisation of everything, regardless of academic disciplines, so much so that some even 'discover' sex and sexuality in things or texts or places that have nothing to do with sex and sexuality. Of course, in some cases sex and sexuality were indeed denied, ignored, concealed, kept secret, forgotten, made to be forgotten and so forth. But such cases are better described as uncovering or recovering rather than discovering sexuality, and queer theory indeed had its work cut out for this in its first decade, investigating the various forms of exclusion of sexuality in history, literature and political economy, to name but a few disciplines. Yet compelling and diverse as they are, these queer critical interventions share an underlying commitment to sexuality (Ferguson 2005: 85), which by now has become a disturbing obsession (Mikdashi and Puar 2016: 221); and to the skeletal form of queer theory's modus operandi – namely, 'queering'. And queering is sexualising, a rose by any other name . . . In short, in this book desexualisation means quite simply challenging sexualisation as the dominant (almost exclusive) form of queering; as well as differentiating between queering and sexualising, and correspondingly, between the two senses of the concept of queer.

To be clear: this book does not amount to a reactionary denunciation of sex or sexuality; I do not try to rob anyone of their sexuality or pleasure. Nor is it an onslaught on queer theory, which has been facing announcements of its 'death', irrelevance, incompetence and whatnot from the beginning (O'Rourke 2011: 103). Quite the contrary – this book is intended as a rebuttal to such claims. Nor will readers find in this book critical discussions about specific sexualities or an attempt to define queerness in relation to this or that sexual identity. Rather, the 'attack' on sexuality in this book proceeds from a Deleuzian critique of queer theory's image of thought, wherein sexuality functions as an unexamined presupposition that depletes the concept of queer of its very 'strangeness' and undermines queer thought's own powers of thinking. Note the distinction between queer theory and queer thought; 'queer theory' is the heterogeneous and multidisciplinary body of knowledge produced by a manner of thinking typical to this field. This manner of thinking is not given but gradually constructed and questioned throughout the book, starting in the next chapter. What I call 'queer thought' is the site where I retrace this manner of thinking, or, in other words, where the question 'What does it mean to think in queer theory?' is posed and deliberated. I find it redundant to parrot the knee-jerk insistence on the so-called plural form of queer theory (and queer thought by

Introduction

extension), which supposedly asserts that there is not one but many queer theories. Is feminist theory or critical race theory any less plural? Is it really a distinct trait of queer theory? On the contrary, the insistence on 'queer theories' is another example of how the sense of queer as indeterminate and strange becomes a determination rendering queer theory well-recognised and intelligible, that is, anything but strange and unknown.

Instead of repeating and reinforcing queer theory's preponderant tendency to sexualise everything, I employ Deleuze's form of critique to investigate the conditions for queer thought's capacity for true novelty and change – first by sorting out what it means to think in queer theory, which explains how queering came to be reduced to sexualisation; and second by asking what can queer theory do beyond sexuality? How could sexuality become a positive and productive point of departure (rather than an end or a foundation) for a critical inquiry?

What is a Deleuzian Critique?

The literature has already established that Deleuze's is a critical philosophy in the tradition of post-Kantianism (Carr 2018; Kerslake 2009; Lundy and Voss 2015). Very broadly, Deleuze's post-Kantianism is expressed in two complementary ways. The first is in qualifications of Deleuze's work as 'a radicalised form of Kantian critical practice' (Carr 2018: 14) or a taking up of the Kantian project 'and carrying it to completion' (Hughes 2012: 28), both of which echo the way Deleuze described Nietzsche's philosophy (NP 52). The second is in the emphasis put in his work on the theme of genesis (of thought or of the faculties, for instance) and its associated demand for a genetic method, which post-Kantians (Deleuze included) regard as a salient function missing from and hence undermining Kant's critical project, and which could be understood as the organising principle of Deleuze's entire oeuvre (Butler 2016: 26; Hughes 2009: 5–6; 2012: 23, 35, 36); or even as an underlying motivation resulting in some of Deleuze's works being regarded as modified doubles of Kant's critical trilogy (Butler 2016: 23).

What I refer to in this book as 'Deleuzian critique' is greatly informed by these studies of Deleuze's post-Kantianism, but my primary interest is more with its actual usage – how is one to use Deleuze's philosophy as a critical tool? To answer that, we need an operational concept of critique in Deleuze that functions at least as a methodological guideline for inquiries bearing a title such as 'a Deleuzian critique of –'. While there are many comments on critique throughout Deleuze's oeuvre (and the scholarship), critique does not enjoy the status of a philosophical concept accorded to other concepts in Deleuze's philosophy (such as assemblage, becoming or intensity). On many occasions Deleuze nevertheless did talk in very practical terms about how he works (mostly in interviews and standalone essays) and in various contexts, ranging from his way of approaching, reading and using the work of other philosophers, to the way he collaborated with Guattari in their actual writing (TRM 237–40), to his practice of watching films for the cinema books (TRM 215–16). There is in all of his writings a tacit yet consistent manner of doing critique, like a spectral procedure always at work beneath the surface of his argumentation, which becomes legible and methodical once it is conceived as a genuine pedagogy, to which Deleuze's own words on teaching apply: 'We learn nothing from those who say: "Do as I do". Our only teachers are those who tell us to "do with me", and are able to emit signs to be developed in heterogeneity' (DR 23). Deleuze himself left us with many such signs (this quote being one of them) in the form of how-to cues or mock instructions that seem to have been taken from a manual or a handbook (such as instructions for building oneself a body without organs in *A Thousand Plateaus*).

I argue that if the different names of Deleuze's methods seem like variations on a single theme, it is due to the coherence of the underlying structure of his critical procedure, which is 'monotonous' in the sense Joe Hughes assigns to the word: 'To affirm Deleuze's monotony is to begin forming the idea of something common across Deleuze's texts by seeking out relations . . . according to the conceptual configurations which lie under Deleuze's variation of names' (2012: 14). I suggest that Hughes's explanation for the transformation of meaning and function of Deleuze's concepts (or their names) throughout his texts applies also to his critical method, which I will describe shortly. This monotony allows us to recognise the operation of the same critical procedure under different names and in different texts, for 'we cannot make connections across [Deleuze's] texts on the basis of a linguistic identity. The identity has to be structural' (Hughes 2012: 22). The same goes for the names of Deleuze's and Deleuze and Guattari's 'disciplines' (TP 43), their systems or method: transcendental empiricism, schizoanalysis, rhizomatics, pragmatics and constructivism, which is the conceptual system chosen for this book (discussed in detail in Chapter 2). From each of them we

Introduction

may extract and analyse the monotonous structure of Deleuzian critique, although once we focus on a given system, the structure of its underlying critical procedure will manifest differently not just in terms of its specific content but also in the role played by the components of that structure – sometimes a particular aspect of the critique receives special attention that the others do not, at other times critique explicitly receives a sense that accentuates or binds to a specific structural element. This is, for example, the case with constructivism in *What is Philosophy?*, where it binds critique to the specific structural element I call 'the problematic'.

What follows is a concise sketch of the structure of Deleuzian critique, which could serve not as a set of principles or rules but as a coherent ensemble of methodological guidelines for doing Deleuzian critique (henceforth simply designated 'critique' unless stated otherwise). If I occasionally describe an element in the form of prescription, the reader should regard it as a mock rule that remains abstract and insufficient unless actively mounted on a specific Deleuzian conceptual system in a defined context. It is also a way to re-present and clarify Deleuze's use of such mock rules, and to understand why we can still learn from them. Concisely, critique is a two-tier procedure, one destructive, the other creative. In terms of practice, the dual nature of this procedure functions as a gateway to what I call the three moments or components of the operational concept of critique, which in turn direct and determine the actual, particular manner by which critique both destroys and creates in a given case. I refer to these three moments as the pragmatic, the problematic and the genetic. A legitimate use of the critique needs to be established each time by two criteria or tests – the test of totality and the test of immanence. Deleuze scholars are familiar with the terms of my description, but recall that my motivation here is to re-examine these terms from the perspective of application so as to derive from Deleuze's work their concrete effect on our use of the critical procedure. Let us now turn to a brief discussion of these elements.

Already in scholastic thought, critique functioned as a two-tiered operation: *pars destruens, pars construens*, which is to say that critique is a procedure both destructive and constructive, negative and affirmative. As Deleuze remarked, 'Critique is destruction as joy, the aggression of the creator' (NP 87). As Michael Hardt noted, Deleuze's own form of critique in his early works maintains this dual structure (1993: 115), though I would argue that it applies to all of his work. The rudimentary function of critique's dual structure is not very different from the Kantian one: in its negative aspect, critique works to eliminate all prejudices and presuppositions about the criticised object so as to clear the path for its affirmative, creative aspect – the construction or constitution of the criticised object in thought in a new, different way, which might have been impossible or unthinkable before, so long as certain biases and presuppositions had determined and constrained our ways of thinking about it. The creative aspect thus necessarily includes the birth (and beginning) of thinking – when thought constructs its object anew in critique, it is already acting against its own habitual ways of thinking and against its own unquestioned presuppositions. The dual structure of critique implies critique's elemental operation each and every time: 'The conditions of a true critique and a true creation are the same: the destruction of an image of thought which presupposes itself and the genesis of the act of thinking in thought itself' (DR 139).

While the two parts of critique may give the impression that each is a moment or phase, which in turn implies a supposedly predetermined chronological order in the execution of critique (first destroy and then create), this is not necessarily the way they are manifested in Deleuze's texts, nor in his actual writing routines.[4] Rather, these two parts coexist in the structure of critique as a whole and in each of three components (which are moments or phases in the same sense) of the concept of critique. This is manifested both concretely and conceptually in Deleuze's work. For example, from a concrete perspective, when one reads *Difference and Repetition*, one could notice that Deleuze's creative conceptual novelty could have benefited from placing the third chapter's critique of the dogmatic image of thought rather at the beginning, before the first two chapters. From a conceptual point of view, the three activities comprising constructivism described in *What is Philosophy?* obey no particular ordering. Note how the argument intimates a practical guideline for the philosopher:

> Each of the three instances is found in the others, but they are not of the same kind, and they coexist and subsist without one disappearing into the other ... [These three activities] continually pass from one to the other, support one another, sometimes precede and sometimes follow each other ... The whole of the problem ... always consists in constructing the other two [activities] when the third is underway. (WP 81)

In other words, constructivism, like Deleuze's other critically formed systems, is dynamic, contingent and multidirectional. Each of critique's components is traversed by its destructive–creative tendency.

Introduction

As a first approximation, the three moments or components of critique can be described concisely as practical rules: the *pragmatic*: tie critique to an external cause; the *problematic*: invent problems and problematise existing solutions; the *genetic*: retrace the genesis of the criticised object to the type of thought in which it was engendered, so as to determine the limits of said thought and thereby to discover unforeseen ways of thinking that express new modes of existence.

The pragmatic moment reveals critique's inherently temporal and political nature, since it links critique to the present – to a non- or extra-philosophical present cause, project or struggle: 'philosophy has an essential relation to time: it is always against its time, critique of the present world' (NP 107). As Buchanan notes, 'none of Deleuze's books are conceived with a purely philosophical objective in mind; there is always a higher, or wider, goal in view, namely the transformation of society' (2000: 32), which is why philosophy for Deleuze 'must do something' (2000: 33). Critique's impetus and *raison d'être* are not to be found in an exercise of speculative reasoning, nor does it originate in some inherent end. The driving force of critique, what sets it in motion, is located outside of it in actual states of affairs and ways of life, and necessarily involves an intentional act executed by the critic. This contact with the outside defines one of the senses of Deleuze and Guattari's functionalism, since they describe it as a guideline orientating both their work and the use of their work by others: 'The question facing every writer is whether or not people have some use ... to make of the book, in their own work, in their life, and in their projects' (TRM 180). In the case of *Anti-Oedipus*, 'our outside', says Deleuze, 'was a particular mass of people ... who are fed up with psychoanalysis' (N 8). *Anti-Oedipus*'s critique of psychoanalysis was not conducted for itself, but was rather designed to ally Deleuze and Guattari with others in their attack, which had already been underway, on its theory and practice. They write for these others and their cause, hoping that their book could serve as an instrument of resistance:

> What matters is whether [*Anti-Oedipus*] works, and how it works, and who it works for ... It's not a matter of reading it over and over again, you have to do something else with it ... We're not writing for people who think psychoanalysis is doing fine ... [but for those] who think it's pretty dull and sad ... We're looking for allies. We need allies. And we think these allies are already out there. (N 22)

Deleuze reiterates his view on the issue of usage, the political aspect of the pragmatic moment, almost every time he talks about books. *Anti-Oedipus*, he says, was not just a book or a book at all:

> We are thinking that it is an element called 'book' in an external set. The worth of the book is not in its interiority, in its pages, but in relation to the multitude of connections outside the book . . . [it refers the reader] to external, political, psychiatric, and psychoanalytic situations. (LOT 199)

Similarly, Deleuze argues that those who follow Foucault do so because his work can be used in their own lives (N 86). The creation of philosophical concepts (the focus of Chapter 2), too, is inseparable from real-life problem to which they respond, and concepts are themselves modes of life and action (TRM 268). Briefly, for critique to function or 'begin' (each of the three moments is a potential beginning), it must be submitted to a pressing concern in the present, to a cause that responds to real problems that is located outside critique.

Moreover, the outside has two distinct yet related senses. I argued that it is the outside that gives critique its purpose and justification, as it links it to a cause; this is the first sense. The second overlaps the first, referring to that which incites thinking, or, more precisely, which forces us to think, for 'thought is primarily trespass and violence' (DR 139). Habitual thinking, or the patterns with which we think, are not acts of thinking for Deleuze. Thinking is not willed but imposed, it begins with absolute passivity and impotence, that is, we begin to think precisely at the very moment we experience the inability of thinking – when our thought faces helplessly something utterly new, be it marvellous or terrifying, but most of all unrecognisable and radically strange. That 'something' is what Deleuze calls a sign – it is the disturbing encounter with a sign that forces us to think: 'What is encountered may be Socrates, a temple or a demon. It may be grasped in a range of affective tones: wonder, love, hatred, suffering. In whichever tone, its primary characteristic is that it can only be sensed' (DR 139). In other words, we experience the powerlessness of thought as a *feeling* that springs up inside us as we encounter something outside ourselves that thought is unable to comprehend or to place in familiar contexts, concepts or images. Yet that something, that imperceptible sign that I can only experience or sense but not recognise, demands to be thought, and this demand takes the form of necessity, an imperative to think that pushes the faculties to their limit, leading them to realise what they can do, their own power (DR 141, 143).

Introduction

The two senses of the outside are related through the necessity and the urgency with which the encounter equips both critique and thought, as well as the new concepts to be created in a genuine act of thinking (DR 139). A cause, a project or a struggle involve practices of resistance to the present that benefit from and are complemented by the practice of critique. These projects may already be themselves the outcome of a preceding encounter, which forced (and thus engendered) the critical thinking that had inspired and led to them; or they could already be underway, and the critique follows for some particular reason, for example, to tackle a new obstacle that existing practices seem unable to overcome, or to rethink an entire project that seems to be corrupted, malfunctioning or degenerating. The pragmatic moment is defined by these two senses of the outside, which provides the critique with the driving force of necessity.

The outside informs the problematic moment of critique, too, no less than it does the pragmatic. The thinking propelled by the encounter with a sign takes the form of problematisation: 'that which can only be sensed ... forces it to pose a problem: as though the object of the encounter, the sign, were the bearer of a problem – as though it were a problem' (DR 140). Nothing is abstract and otherworldly about such thinking because it was 'never just a theoretical matter. It was to do with vital problems. To do with life itself' (N 105). Now, Deleuze's concept of the problem deserves an elaborate, thoughtful account that befits its import and complexity, which it has received in the literature. Here I rather focus on its taking the dynamic form of a process (namely, problematisation), and its practical implications for critique. In an interview incredibly rich in how-to cues and mock instructions, Deleuze seamlessly weaves the problematic moment with the other two, as he implicitly relates them to the inward sensation of that something outside of us that violently forces us to think. Although Deleuze often describes this force as the intolerable, we should recall that it need not necessarily be a negative sensation. Encounters may also effect an intense feeling of joy, love and admiration (the last two are related, as I will explain shortly). This is especially true, apparently, if one is to critique another great thinker:

> When you're facing such a work of a genius, there's no point saying you disagree. First you have to know how to admire; you have to rediscover the problems [a thinker] poses, his particular machinery. *It is by the force of admiration that you will come to genuine critique ...* You have to

work your way back to those problems which an author of genius has posed, all the way back to that which he does not say *in* what he says, in order to extract something that still belongs to him, though you also turn it against him. You have to be inspired, visited by the geniuses you denounce. (DI 139, translation modified; my emphasis)

Critique, like genuine thinking, begins with pathos, it affects the body. Interestingly, however, admiration is not just some familiar spontaneous feeling one supposedly already has, but a know-how, or, in other words, an effect of learning. How do you learn to admire? You retrace the problems that occupy a thinker's work to discover in its silences something utterly new that, at the same time, has been there all along, rightfully belonging to the thinker. Retracing problems in this paradoxical manner means inventing or constructing them, as Deleuze famously said, for it involves the creative power of critique – the problem must be invented, for it is not simply 'there' in the work. Reaching these problems is a humbling learning experience – it earns one's admiration, which nonetheless does not compromise one's critical motivation; on the contrary, it is only then that one is truly capable of critiquing ('turn it against him').

Once you notice Deleuze talking about his admiration for other thinkers, you discover that it is all over his interviews and essays, always in reference to thinkers he wrote about, and always using the verb *admirer* except on a few occasions where he uses the verb *aimer* (to love). There is no strict differentiation between admiring, loving and fucking for Deleuze. They are interchangeable because they all bear a non-sexual sense slightly varying in degree: 'through someone, what we love is non personal, on the order if fluxes that pass or don't pass', said Deleuze (LOT 216), and this sentiment resonates in his description of his meetings with Guattari in the famous 'Letter to a Harsh Critic': 'the way we understood and complemented, depersonalized and singularized – in short, loved – one another' (N 7). While problems seem to originate in the personal life of a thinker, they refer to ways of life, modes of existence and types of thinking that are not subjective but collective, and they respond to a sign in the present as they enable reaching for the future, because the thinker is inseparable from a people to come (WP 109).

Once we realise that when Deleuze talks about his admiration and love for Guattari, Foucault (N 4, 102, 150), Blanchot (N 30) or others the real object of his love is the impersonal and the problematic in their work, even the most erotic or sexually explicit passages in

Deleuze's texts reveal their non-sexual sense. Compare, for example, the passage quoted above (about admiring as a retracing back to a thinker's problem) to Deleuze's famous description of the history of philosophy as a buggery or immaculate conception:

> I saw myself taking an author from behind and giving him a child that would be his own offspring, yet monstrous. It was really important for it to be his own child, because the author had to actually say all I had him saying. But the child was bound to be monstrous too, because it resulted from all sorts of shifting, slipping, dislocations, and hidden emissions that I really enjoyed. (N 6)

Deleuze, in my reading of this passage, loves or fucks that which is problematic and impersonal in the thinkers he wrote about, regardless of their or his sexuality. Problematising is a form of asexual reproduction – it creates something new, a new life or a new possibility of living; it is a form of lovemaking not with actual persons and genitals, but with the virtual ideas and problems of other thinkers. This also explains Deleuze's curious remark about sodomy amounting to immaculate conception – what matters is not the sexual nature of his relation to other thinkers, but rather the capacity to create something new out of an essentially sterile interaction. The monstrous child born out of the unholy union is that very same something unsaid (mentioned in the previous passage) that Deleuze eventually finds in what a thinker says by way of problematisation – something that 'still belongs to him' though used against him (which offers another explanation for the child's monstrosity). It is unsurprising, then, that taking the author as a whole, another famous how-to by Deleuze, also involves admiration and retracing-constructing problems (N 85–6).

The problematic moment of critique is what allows it to both problematise solutions and create a problem (B 35), a procedure originating from and immanent to life itself (B 16). One problematises solutions by revealing them to be responding to false problems, a move that enables one to construct a new problem that could be pronounced true by making sure its determination is a function of its immanent use (Wasser 2017: 56). The two senses of problematisation are inseparable, for they both involve an immanent screening process separating (that is, determining) true from false problems, and critique is designed to provide the means for this process (DR 168). The process of screening has important practical implications, for it guides critique to the particular manner of thinking that created it, and thus allows the creative aspect of critique to be activated. False problems are 'a retrograde movement of thought, in that it ushers in decisions about what is supposed to be up for debate ... [they are] a restrictive construct, in that it limits possible responses to those which have agreed in advance to the terms of the question' (Wasser 2017: 58).

There is no single, predetermined way to distinguish true from false problems; there are in fact many ways to do this, none of which can be decided in advance, for they are identified by and discussed in terms belonging to a specific situation or encounter. This is why, for example, Deleuze finds that in Kant, false problems refer to illegitimate uses of ideas (DR 168), but in Bergson, they refer to 'the order of general ideas that tends to obscure differences in kind' (B 33). In terms of the argument I have presented so far, we can describe a false problem as 'that which is not a problem, that which does not testify to any genuine act of problematization: the absence of any encounter or relation with the outside' (Zourabichvili 2012: 64). A true problem, on the other hand, appears when thought is violently forced to think as it encounters the outside. It is the contingency of the encounter that endows a problem with its necessity and truth (DR 145).

We rediscover the problematic moment's relation to the present when we critique what seem like failed solutions, but in so doing what we are actually saying, according to Deleuze, is that the problem has changed – it is not our problem any more, and therefore its existing solution appears irrelevant, insignificant or failed. Again, this is not something that occurs before or after one has posited a problem, because these are the two faces of the same process, namely, problematisation. The problematic moment provides the critic with useful practical tools: the encounter with the outside causes one to sense that a new problem has appeared – something that one's habitual ways of thinking are unable to recognise. That is the critic's first cue, since that unrecognisable something takes the form of a problem for thought as it begins to think – this is the genesis of the act of thinking in thought, which sets in motion the constructing of the conditions of the problem. The first cue is inseparable from another, which is also perceived as a felt effect – the critic experiences a new measure of distance from existing solutions, a feeling that ranges from indifference to alienation and resentment. This is simply the other expression of the feeling that this is not our problem any more, the event of thinking: 'something has happened, "the problem has changed". We can celebrate it or deplore it, we can cling to the old problematic, but

Introduction

it imposes itself nevertheless as *our* problem, since it elicits creation' (Zourabichvili 2012: 90).

Realising that the problem has changed, that existing solutions are inadequate, and that a new problem needs to be invented leads us to the genetic moment of critique. The post-Kantian demand for a genetic method is translated into a practical task – to account for the genesis of the very act of thinking that began in the encounter with the unrecognisable new, that moment when thought met its limits. In other words, we are looking for the image of thought to which particular problems and solutions are immanent, and which will in turn allow us to understand that thought's power to transform itself, since this power is not added to thought from without but rather exists within it in the form of potential. Only at the limits of thought can we come up with new alternative solutions to the new problem we encounter, for thought's limit 'refers to that on the basis of which [a thing] is deployed and deploys all its power' (DR 37).

Nous autres, *Queers*

In what sense are we no longer queer? And who is this *we*? I use this pronoun in a fairly simple sense – *we* are 'others to queer' and the 'other queers' for whom the concept of queer is lost or severely compromised; *we* who find ourselves incapable of thinking queerly any more or who have grown numb and somewhat weary of queer thought in its dominant, institutionalised forms (such as deconstruction or anti-normativity). And it is of course *we* who are profoundly in need of a genuine act of queer thinking and a spark of queer novelty because something in our lives, in our present, is intolerable and we need allies and new critical tools that work for us. This book suggests that Deleuze's philosophy could be just that, which means that it could help us understand what queer theory can do and what it could become. This is not a book for those who are happy with queer theory the way it is, and certainly not for those who criticise it not so as to make it better, but to be done with it. Some of those critics can even bring themselves to write a whole book just to condemn queer theory, in the hope that their pronouncing it dead would kill it (see the next chapter for a discussion of such critics).

We are no longer queer because the problem has changed; it is not our problem any more. Queer was always much more than just a word; later I will argue for conceiving it as a philosophical concept, and a rare one. I argue that like every philosophical concept, queer was created as a solution to a problem, as an urgent response born out of a dire necessity – in this case, the AIDS crisis in the 1980s and 1990s in the United States – but rarely has it been acknowledged as essentially such a response. Of course, no one working in queer theory denies the concept's relation to the AIDS crisis, but very few have given serious consideration to what made queer imperative, or how it was to solve the problem of the crisis. It is not only introductions to queer theory that have propagated this oversight, as will be discussed in the next chapter. It is as if queer theory had altogether severed its ties with the conditions of the problem that breathed new life into the old slur, making it a powerful tool of resistance, even as AIDS transformed into a global pandemic, that is, a new problem affecting other places around the globe, beyond the West, where AIDS is still very much a death threat. In other words, detached from its problem, queer thought had been separated from its own powers early on to become a one-trick pony that submitted diverse objects to a single process – queering, that is, sexualising. Put differently, queer theory became an uncritical or partial form of critique, which unwittingly elevated sexuality to a transcendent instance. In so doing it surrendered both its difference from gay and from its own internal difference, its defining character, its powers.

In conclusion, here is a recapitulation of this book's main points in the form of short theses, which weave together the introduction's arguments and critical terminology with the arguments comprising the next chapters:

Queer is an American phenomenon. The fact that the term queer is employed in new and global contexts in the scholarship may give the false impression that queer is universal. This illusion is an effect of queering qua sexualising, which effectively made queer an identity term. Barring purposeful conceptualisation, queer usually bears no considerable significance or weight in the scholarly texts that employ it, as it carries the same loose sense in this scholarship, namely, it refers to any non-normative sexuality. The birth of queer in the US is the contingency without which all concepts 'lack the claws of absolute necessity' (DR 139), since the US determined the conditions that allowed queer to then transform from a slur to a concept. In other words, the US provided the environment for the violent chance encounter of thought with the outside.

The concept of queer was born as a response to the AIDS crisis. It was not created out of whim or a playful postmodern attitude towards sexual identity, nor was it simply the fruit of an elitist

Introduction

and obnoxiously cryptic academic thinking that concocted it in the ivory tower. My contention is that understanding the power, use and significance of the concept requires a shift in focus from grounding the concept in histories of sexuality and poststructuralist theories to retracing the geophilosophical conditions of the problem to which queer responds as a solution. This shift entails a renewed examination of the AIDS crisis in its most direct relationship with the concept of queer, for the crisis plays the role of the sign in the encounter: AIDS had to become 'an unbearable idea' (Crimp 2002: 227), that is, it became the name of a problem that, prior to its formal naming, manifested itself in the sensation of the intolerable or the unthinkable that forces thought to think – the shock responsible for the genesis of queer thought. AIDS was literally unrecognisable in the first years of the crisis, inflicting violence not only on thought but also on the body and the self. Of course, it is not hard to imagine the crisis as the intolerable since it was conceived as a death sentence from the beginning. But I would venture to say that it is AIDS as a sign in the encounter which is responsible for its becoming an 'epidemic of signification' (Treichler 1999: 19). Queer as a concept is a response to the crisis in the sense that it originates in the realisation according to which 'AIDS does not exist apart from the practices that conceptualize it, represent it, and respond to it. We know AIDS only through these practices' (Crimp 2002: 28), all the more so since 'there is no reason that explains AIDS . . . but there is meaning' (Bordowitz 2004: 48).

Queer is defined by its internal difference. There is irony in that queer's power to debilitate fixed meanings and identities turned into a domesticated affirmation of identity. As discussed in the next chapter, the sense of queer's indeterminacy is transposed on to sexuality, and sexuality will be thus rediscovered, again and again, as the principle of coherence and unity of any 'queered' object, since sexuality tacitly acquires the status of a foundation or a first principle to which all differences refer, and which therefore renders them derivative. To queer something means rendering it indeterminate, but this indeterminacy is already generalised in the notion of sexuality as a 'true' form of difference. Queer's internal difference originates in the tension between its two senses that keeps them inseparable yet distinct. Once sexuality assuaged this tension by taming the indeterminate, queer lost its indeterminacy and its critical edge. And queer theory thus became respectable, friendly, institutionalised and mostly devoid of revolutionary power.

Revisioning queer's internal difference means two things: first, a critical inquiry is required to retrace the process described above, by which queer's internal difference came to be covered over by sexuality. Second, it is necessary to retell the story of its emergence as a response to the AIDS crisis, which leads to a second perspective on queer's internal difference, namely, capturing its coexistence in three different domains that thereby had become interrelated: political activism (the ACT UP movement), academia (queer theory) and the arts, particularly cinema (New Queer Cinema). Queer's non-philosophical beginning was in the streets, and in collective feelings of anger, grief, shame, fear and exhaustion, from which nonetheless burst an explosive and contagious affirmation of life. As former ACT UP activist, artist and scholar Gregg Bordowitz clarifies, 'the single most important objective is to affirm the lives of people living with AIDS and the social relations these lives include' (2004: 34–5). In Chapter 3, I argue that activists and artists were much more sensitive to and perceptive of queer's true revolutionary power to affirm life in the face of death, desperation and indifference to life, than were queer theorists.

Notes

1. See Kedem 2019.
2. There are, of course, impressive yet very rare works that successfully bring together Deleuze's philosophy with queer theory without falling into the trap of sexualisation. A recent study brilliantly connects Deleuze with posthumanist theory and queer negativity (a concept that refers to the framework of the antisocial turn in queer theory) to argue for an ethics based on the impersonal and the dissolution of the self that is nevertheless affirmative of life (Swarbrick 2019).
3. In translations of Foucault's work into English, *dispositif* is sometimes translated as 'device', 'deployment' or 'apparatus', none of which captures all the senses at work in this concept. See Agamben's discussion of these senses (2009: 2–3).
4. Deleuze's description of how Guattari and he worked together on their mutual projects could serve as an example for his non-linear manner of writing. See TRM 237–40; D 16–17.

1
Queer Theory's Image of Thought

It might seem odd to argue that the question 'What is queer?' has rarely been posed. After all, does the extensive body of scholarly work known as 'queer theory' not begin with this very question, and is it not at pains to maintain at least some sense of 'queer' as a theoretical concept, disparate and elusive as it might be? We hear it again and again, *ad nauseam*: queer is a term not fully determined, and necessarily so. Something about queer always eludes and remains beyond reach, but not as excess; on the contrary, '[queer's] definitional indeterminacy, its elasticity, is one of its constituent elements' (Jagose 1996: 1). Moreover, 'the great virtue of "queer" lay precisely in its undefinability, which included a certain unpredictability in the implications and consequences of deploying the concept' (Turner 2000: 146). The semantic history of the word, as suggested by Jagose's use of 'indeterminate', reveals queer to be that which is strange, that is, unknown, unfamiliar, unaccountable. In the early 1910s queer also became a derogatory term for homosexuals, and this semantic link between the strange and the homosexual was later utilised productively by queer theory, activism and art in the 1980s and 1990s in the United States – particularly against the negative value assigned to it as a derogatory term.[1] Accounts of queer theory often include definitions of 'queer', but almost always reluctantly and apologetically: reluctantly, because any definition – by definition – is essentially an imposition of limits that allows stable meanings to emerge, hence rendering the proclaimed 'indeterminate' knowable and determinate; apologetically, because definitions are presumed to be inevitable if one is to make any sense of a vast, widely heterogeneous scholarship (theory) that takes 'queer' (the indeterminate) as its qualifier.

Why insist on the concept's inherent indeterminacy, if the theory to which queer is attached as a qualifier ends up being a determinate theory of sexuality? Queer theory seems to be entangled in a paradox: on the one hand, qualifying theory as queer was intended to disrupt habitual, conventional or traditional ways of thinking, that is, to transform no less than thought itself. Lisa Duggan argues that queer holds 'the promise of new meanings, new ways of thinking and acting politically' (2001: 215). As such, it seems that queer theory always aspires to think novelty and change and to align itself with similar-minded critical projects. For Noreen Giffney, queer theory offers a promising way of thinking the unthinkable that is very much akin to Deleuze and Guattari's thought (2009: 9), while Steven Seidman defines the operations of queer theory in terms of Derrida's famous concept of deconstruction (1997: xi). Thomas Dowson pinpoints the political value of disrupting thought by means of queering it when he accounts for the need to use queer theory in archaeology: 'queering archeology empowers us to think what is often the unthinkable to produce unthought-of pasts. Those pasts, those queer archaeologies, allow subordinate groups a voice in constructing their past' (Dowson 2000: 165). Many insist that queer qualifies theory as a practice rather than a determinable system of applicable and representable ideas; as a question of doing, rather than being – a critical, disruptive and deconstructive mode of thinking that is set against thought's own habitual ways of organising experience according to normative standards.

On the other hand, that same practice of critical thinking seems to qualify thought itself as essentially sexual: first in the sense that, in Judith Butler's words, it takes sexuality as its 'proper object' (1997: 4–5). Queer theory thus becomes a theory *of* sexuality that is not so much a disruptive force of critical thinking as it is a critique of normativity that is defined in sexual terms (such as hetero- or homonormativity) – a move that scholars working in queer theory would later find to be problematic and limiting.[2] In other words, if one is to be critical of normative thinking by means of reaching the unthought or the new, it also seems that one is required to uncover and challenge the supposed sexual nature of normative thinking. Such a critical move, then, does not question the sexual nature of thought itself, but only what it considers to be thought's problematic, (sexually) normative manifestation. Nor does it wish to do away with sexuality altogether; on the contrary, it finds more and more ways of thinking of and *as* a sexual being – from reconceptualising the more familiar categories such as bisexuality and transgenderism, to engaging with new forms of sexuality such as intersexuality, asexuality, non-binary, pansexuality and others. For a recently published volume that attempts to rethink queer theory's relationship with psychoanalysis, these presuppositions regarding thought's sexual nature have become non-problematic: the concept of queer is all about sexuality, queer theory is pronounced a sub-field of sexuality studies and is utilised for challenging thinking itself if it betrays a bias towards hetero- or homosexuality (Giffney 2017: 30).

Second and consequently, thought is discovered to be essentially sexual even in thinkers who do not presuppose its sexual nature or are not exclusively concerned with sexuality. For instance, risking conceptual anachronism, Verena Conley considers both Derrida's and Deleuze and Guattari's works as always-already queer ways of thinking in both senses of queer: a thought that 'makes strange' *and* that experiments with homosexuality (2009: 24–5). Kemp relies on Deleuze's famous description of philosophy as buggery to argue that 'philosophy, according to Deleuze, is always already a queer practice, a question of taking past thinkers from behind', and consequently, to suggest that 'a profoundly erotic mode of engagement emerges at the heart of western thinking' (2009: 151). Although the sexual nature of thought rarely appears as an explicit presupposition, I contend that it can always be deduced from any description of queer theory that insists on both its inherent power to disrupt (to render strange, indeterminate) *any* normative thinking, and at the same time on its definitive objective – to unsettle the fundamental (hetero- or homo-) sexual normativity of thought that supposedly underlies any field. In other words, thought appears to be inherently sexual every time queer theory confuses its particular, easily definable operation (as a critique of sexual normativity) with a universal model of critical thinking as such (an indeterminate force of disruptive thinking that is able to transform thought), rather than regarding itself as a case of critical thinking. Only if it presupposes the sexual nature of thought can queer theory lay claim to both the particular and the universal, and perceive itself as both inherently indeterminate and guided in principle by a sexually determinable object. The reason is that such a presupposition forms more than simply a direct relation between thought and sexuality; it also establishes a resemblance between thought's critical function – its power to transcend the empirical and to engender the new or reach the unthought – and sexuality's supposed inherent indeterminacy, that is, its constitutive perversity that either undermines normative sexual identities or inheres in them as their potential to disintegrate or transform into something new.

Perhaps this would not have been problematic if queer theory was satisfied with revolutionising only sexual thought or sexual politics – that is, if it only promised us new ways to think *of* sexuality rather than claiming to revolutionise thought as such, or to be the 'true' manifestation of revolutionary thought. But queer theory's ambitious claim led many of its critics to see it as a new dogmatism and elitism. More recent studies lead to an even further, somewhat paradoxical theoretical consequence: while queer theorists insist on the concept's inherent strangeness, once it qualifies 'theory' that same theory is made known and knowable, perhaps even to the point of its own exhaustion. In his *After Queer Theory*, James Penney opens his account with the firm assertion that 'queer discourse has run its course, its project made obsolete by the full elaboration of its own logic' (2014: 1). As the book's title clearly suggests, Penney's interest lies in moving away from and beyond queer theory's dominant tendencies (which he rigorously criticises and often rejects), and in forming new, politically enabling theoretical connections with Marxism and psychoanalysis in order to rethink 'the place of sexuality in transformative political thought' (2014: 8).[3] Less definitively, but no less critical of queer theory's limited scope, David V. Ruffolo argued that queer theory reached a political peak due to the privileged currency it had assigned to the queer/heteronormative dyad – a dead-ended, unfailingly self-reproducing binarism, which resulted in investigations centred upon processes of subjectification and their corresponding conceptualisations of the body that mark their fixed (hence exhausted) political horizon (Ruffolo 2009: 381; 2016: 4–5, 20).

Both Penney and Ruffolo meticulously unravel what they consider to be the dead ends that inevitably led to queer theory's demise. The difference between their accounts can be roughly described as a difference in orientation: Penney criticises queer theory *from without* in the sense that his investigation is constructed as a joint Marxist-psychoanalytic critique of both early fundamental assumptions and current trends and concerns of queer theory. Ruffolo, on the other hand, critiques queer theory *from within* in the sense that his investigation is constructed as a series of critical peaks that demonstrates both queer theory's limits and potential. For instance, both Penney and Ruffolo are critical of queer theory's heavy reliance on the notion of hetero- and homonormativity. But for Penney what invalidates this notion is, from a Marxist point of view, queer theory's indifference to the current mode of production, and, generally, its refusal to historicise itself (2014: 15, 64, 72); and, from a psychoanalytical point of view, queer theory's 'unpersuasive' interpretation of the Lacanian Real as that which naturalises heterosexuality (2014: 47, 49–55). For Ruffolo, on the contrary, this notion marks queer theory's internal limit, since it is structured as a binarism (either heteronormative or queer) that itself presupposes – and is thus restrictive to begin with – the primacy of language and discourse (or of categories of representation and signification) for the intelligibility of subjectivities and bodies (2016: 15, 17–23). Their choosing of 'after' and 'post' for the titles of their works is telling in this respect; according to Penney, queer theory in its current state is 'dead' because it has failed to address the role of the socio-economic material conditions of our experience of our own sexuality, and because it embraces misreadings of Freud and Lacan. Thus, he positions himself after (and obviously outside) queer theory. Ruffolo's 'post-queer', alternatively, does not so much mark a complete departure or detachment from queer theory, as aim to explore its creative potential to transform itself and go beyond its current scope while retaining relations with what queer theory has been and done thus far (2016: 30).

Both studies attest to a reality in which queer theory – despite queer's constitutive indeterminacy that supposedly safeguards the openness of theory and therefore its transformative potential and availability for application in varying fields – has come to signify a recognisable body of knowledge that is anything but indeterminate. Therefore, some find it futile, if not utterly false or naïve, to insist on queer theory's inherent indeterminacy, particularly as that which holds the promise of a radical, progressive, political thought. For example, Sheila Jeffreys' *Unpacking Queer Politics* represents a vehement attack on queer theory's promise of radical politics. Queer theory's 'predilection' for the deconstruction of identity and uncritical espousing of transgression as a political means has led, she argues, to the exclusion of lesbian feminists and bisexuals from both activist movements and theoretical work. The enticing, all-inclusive yet indeterminate term 'queer' suffers from a 'masculine bias' (Jeffreys 2003: 42), and, as a form of politics, was founded upon 'the repudiation of the ideas of lesbian feminism' (2003: 57); it is thus nothing but a smokescreen that serves to advocate the rights and needs of gay men, and to provide 'theoretical justification for a series of specifically male practices . . . [which have been] the object of critique in gay liberation and feminist theory' (2003: 55).[4]

Mis-introductions

The problem of defining 'queer' is nowhere more evident today than in sympathetic introductions to queer theory, all the more so since introducing this concept seems to entail a specification of the stakes associated with the problem of defining queer as well as possible ways to handle them. Jagose opens her introductory account by suggesting that any attempt to introduce 'the queer phenomenon' may be self-defeating, 'for part of queer's semantic clout, part of its political efficacy, depends on its resistance to definition' (1996: 1). She then quickly points out the stakes: to identify 'queer theory' as a school of thought and as an object of attainable knowledge means 'to risk domesticating it, and fixing it in ways that queer theory resists fixing itself' (1996: 2). To avoid such fixation, she offers instead a map of the mobile, often contradictory, tendencies within queer theory and queer identifications; one that situates them in the context of the history of sexual categories, while maintaining queer's 'sense of potentiality that it cannot yet quite articulate' (1996: 2). For Jagose, one must refrain from saying the last word on queer if queer is to live up to its 'radical potential' as a critical term (1996: 6).

While its critical power as a concept may be more than a matter of semantics, as a qualifier of theory queer implies a paradox resonating with the one discussed above. On the one hand, queer marks a plural theory characterised by indeterminacy, which is thus predisposed to regain new, constantly changing contexts and uses. On the other hand, it also marks a theory that is bound to sexuality as its object (indeterminate as it might claim to be). As an object of theory, sexuality comes to define queer theory's scope, as well as its distribution of means, ends and presuppositions (indeterminate and ever-changing as they might be). Put differently, while the indeterminate sense of queer marks a theory that refuses any referential function that might compromise its critical openness, its sexual sense nevertheless tethers theory to an identifiable object or referent – be it the category of sexuality or the lived experience of sexualised subjects – that predetermines and diminishes theory's possibilities for critical application. What theory *can* do (a theory *that* queers) becomes, then, inevitably dependent upon the question of what theory *is* (a theory *of* queers).

This ambivalence between what queer (and queer theory) can do and what queer is articulates the stakes of queer's conceptual power in Nikki Sullivan's introduction to queer theory. Defining what queer is, Sullivan contends, 'would be a decidedly un-queer thing to do' (2003: 43). She offers instead a review of multiple definitions made by different authors to suggest that the plurality of definitions indicates queer's lack of conceptual stability or fixed identity. More importantly, Sullivan shows that both assigning *and* refusing to assign queer an identity inevitably lead to theoretical dead ends and grave political consequences, such as a misleading sense of inclusivity, a reproduction of the exclusionary logic of identity politics, and even a possibly abusive use of the term to legitimise questionable sexual practices. Perhaps 'it may be more productive to think of queer as verb (a set of actions), rather than as a noun (an identity, or even a nameable positionality)', she says. Thus, in her reading 'queer' comes to stand for a 'deconstructive practice' (2003: 50) or 'strategy' (2003: 52): one that analyses the specific ways in which heterosexuality and homosexuality as hierarchised binary oppositions have been developed and reproduced throughout history in varying contexts (2003: 51).

At this point we can already present a provisional explanation as to why the question 'What is queer?' has rarely been posed: introductions to 'queer theory' explicitly un/define 'queer' only to rediscover its sense in 'queer theory' by rendering the questions 'What is queer?' and 'What is queer theory?' interchangeable, as if we can only make sense of 'queer' as a critical term – determine how it works, what it can do, how it can be used or applied, and in which contexts – by referring it to 'queer theory'. Before expanding on this point further, it should be noted that this problem is not confined to introductory books on or articles about queer theory, nor is it a problem of introductions as such; it is rather the problem of introducing or thinking radical, irreducible difference. If we are to account for the difference that 'queer' as a concept makes – how it is different in each and every case, how it can be plugged into changing contexts and problems to effect change; how 'queer theory' and 'queer activism', for instance, come to designate 'the promise of new meanings, new ways of thinking and acting politically' (Duggan 2001: 215) – without relinquishing queer's proclaimed indeterminacy, its transformative potential or its strategic value, we need to devise the means to think differently and to think difference. Later I will argue that thinking queer in terms of radical difference is the task of a Deleuzian critique, here as the underlying procedure of constructivism. The first step for such a critique is to wrest the concept from the grasp of queer thought, and it begins here – where I suggest that displacing the question 'What is queer?' – or, what amounts to the same thing, deflating the conceptual power of queer – occurs in two interrelated moves: from signification to significance, and from significance to signification.

From signification to significance: the conceptual power of queer is never ascribed to simple definitions, but rather to its value or import. Queer, then, must become more than a word or a sign if we are to understand why and how it makes a difference. Linguistic signs in themselves tell us nothing of their value for they are but the arbitrary relation of signifier and signified. Language as a system of signs is established on a principle of equivalence: no sign is superior or inferior to another sign, for, as signs, they are all interchangeable in principle. Semiotics, then, cannot tell us why queer matters, nor account for its critical power. It is here that we first see how queer acquires value only by being reduced to a qualifier of theory, in a seamless move from sign to concept. Introductions are exemplary of this sort of move when they cite or discuss various definitions of the elusive queer, which in actuality are attributed to 'queer theory'. Sullivan begins with 'some fairly typical explanations of queer' and concludes that same paragraph with 'Queer (Theory) is constructed as a sort of vague and indefinable set of practices and (political) positions that has the potential to challenge normative knowledges and identities' (Sullivan 2003: 43–4). Here the indeterminate sense of queer smoothly comes to bear upon the bracketed 'Theory', equating what queer as a concept can do with what queer theory can do. Similarly, Jagose wavers between 'queer phenomenon' and 'queer theory' and 'queer identification', only to argue eventually that 'while there is no critical consensus on the definitional limits of queer . . . [it] describes those gestures or analytical models which dramatize incoherencies in the allegedly stable relations between chromosomal sex, gender and sexual desire' (Jagose 1996: 3). To account for its significance, then, queer is reduced to a qualifier that seems to make sense only as a component of a different term, namely, queer theory.

From significance to signification: once brought under the reins of queer theory, queer retains its indeterminate sense only as an empty gesture that obscures the resurrection of its referential function. We saw how queer gains value or significance by way of its being detached from semantics and semiotics, making its indeterminate sense a qualifier of theory that supposedly guarantees theory's continued openness and critical power. Now it gains value by way of surrendering the indeterminate sense to the sexual one, so that queer in fact – and despite all claims to the contrary – is made to refer back to an identifiable object. It is now the object that is plural, indeterminate and evasive, be it sexuality as a category (ontological, epistemological, political, cultural etc.), or as the lived experience of embodied subjects (gays, lesbians, transgenders, bisexuals etc.). Introductions are partially to blame for this move because they, in a sense, only reproduce the theoretical moves already at work in the texts that comprise what they refer to as queer theory. But in another sense, introductions are responsible for perfecting it to the point of abstraction, which in turn intensifies the signifying function of the concept. With undoubtedly the best pedagogical intentions in mind and for obvious reasons, introducers of queer theory feel compelled to contextualise queer by embedding it in a historical narrative. While it cannot be disputed that a concept has a history and that it acquires significance under actual circumstances, at the hands of introducers the conceptual power (what the concept can mean or do) is derived from (and reduced to) its historical actualisations (its past meanings and uses). The concept is then implanted into the same contextualising narrative again and again – in the evolution of sexuality studies as it relates to feminist and gay and lesbian studies and politics, as if the one and the same context could account for the multiplicity of its senses and usages in other contexts too, such as 'queer activism' and 'queer cinema'. It is unclear, then, how and in what sense queer as a concept can be related critically to other contexts without concurrently rediscovering their supposedly inherent sexual character; nor is it clear how it could acquire any new sense that resists reproducing and falling back on the 'rediscovered' always-already sexualised nature of the object being queered.[5]

For example, far into her introduction, after having devoted no less than five chapters to the history of sexuality studies and politics, and only after reviewing the 'infiltration' of poststructuralism into American academia, Jagose states: 'if post-structuralist theory can be claimed as part of the context of queer, then queer's emergence as a diacritical term can be linked just as plausibly ... [to] the network of activism and theory generated by the AIDS epidemic' (1996: 93). Jagose summarises that which is admittedly regarded as an equally important historical context for considerations of queer, in a series of general points and issues ripped from the specificity of their respective contexts, and then briefly explains how these generalities parallel or relate to issues in queer theory in a loose, barely three-page-long account.

Similarly, Sullivan excuses herself altogether from discussing the meaning of queer other than the ways it informs queer theory, despite, by her own admission, the senses of queer created in other contexts having played a formative role in the emergence of queer theory:

> whilst it is important to acknowledge the existence of a range of queer activist groups such as ACT UP, Queer Nation, [and] OutRage ... that formed in the 1990s and shaped Queer Theory and its practice, it is not within the bounds of this chapter to discuss these groups ... in any detail. (2003: 37)

'Queering' other contexts, then, will be formulated in her subsequent discussion as always resembling, 'resonating with' or 'sharing' the strategy of queer theory. So, for example, when she discusses what it could mean to queer the notion of community, Sullivan first reviews various conceptualisations of community, and after discussing Nancy's version of the concept she concludes: 'one could claim that this notion of community as a fracturing or undoing shares resonances with the way we have been thinking about queer as a deconstructive strategy that denaturalises heteronormative identities, relations, and institutions' (2003: 148). Concisely, this argument demonstrates that seamless, circular move from signification to significance and back again that I have been outlining thus far: queer is not just a word, but a deconstructive strategy (although it is in fact queer theory that Sullivan described earlier as such); but as such, it is not even the fleeting process or practice Derrida described, but rather one assigned with a specific task and object – the denaturalisation of heteronormative identities, values and so on.[6]

By comparison, Donald E. Hall's *Queer Theories* can be said to offer a more cautious, self-aware treatment of the conceptualisation of queer and its potential for critical applications, but due to an insistent emphasis on sexuality, queer's conceptual power remains firmly attached to its object. Hall opens with a full disclosure of his own presuppositions, which he summarises in eight brief principles. The first four link the concept of queer to the problems and history of sexuality, identity and their theorisation. The last four address the importance of maintaining a critical, self-aware theoretical practice (including his own), and the future of queer theory. He then turns to review 'working definitions' of queer – three distinct definitions that are informed by their grammatical function: queer as an adjective (the plural quality of queerness that challenges any fixed, single qualification of identity), a noun (the derogatory proper name that designates actual queer beings) and a verb (the act of disturbing dominant value systems that determine the difference between the normal and the abnormal) (Hall 2003: 12–14).

Queer Theory's Image of Thought

Although Hall takes his cue from Michael Warner's broader definition of queer – for whom queer stands for 'a thorough resistance to regimes of the normal' (Warner 1993: xxvi) – to advocate an open-ended use of the concept and an argument for the plurality of queer theories, his eight principles and the relations he forms between the three definitions nevertheless compromise his otherwise critical treatment of the concept. The first four principles emphasise the role that sexuality plays in conceptualising queer. Queer theories, therefore, even in their plural form, always seem to relate to other contexts either by sexualising them (in the form of a critique of transparent yet imposed heteronormative values), or by bringing the emphasised category of sexuality to bear on other identity categories such as race, class, gender and so forth. But even more problematic is the naturalisation of the affinity between the noun, adjective and verb forms of queer implied in Hall's move from describing the historical formation of a reactionary concern in the twentieth century – the public worry according to which 'queers' (noun), who are characterised by their abnormal sexuality, might somehow spread their dangerous 'queerness' (adjective) – to arguing that this concern found its affirmative and strategic counter-realisation in 'queering' (verb), which was reclaimed against 'systems of classification [of sexuality and other identity categories] that assert their timelessness and fixity' (Hall 2003: 14). This move does not do justice to Hall's otherwise careful conceptualisation of queer, which denies any fixed essence or nature to either queerness or queering. As in the previous cases of contextualising queer described above, Hall's account unwittingly makes a historical contingency (the actual circumstances under which the relation of queer to sexuality had been formed) into a definitive context that determines and restricts queer's conceptual power – its celebrated malleability and its irreducible self-difference, which can presumably enable the creation of new values by disrupting established ones without reducing or surrendering its own difference to any of them. Hall's 'queer theories' therefore inevitably reach their limit because his critical consideration of queer as a concept never does away with sexuality altogether, but rather narrows down the concept's scope in accordance with a presupposed sexual context. Consequently, much like other introducers of queer theory, Hall ends up reproducing the same restrictive sense of queer. For example, his description of the project of queering intellectual history reads much like Sullivan's account of queering popular culture, namely, as one that recovers 'telling traces of the "abnormal" even among "normal" (canonical, *heterosexual*) philosophers and theorists' (Hall 2003: 56). Queering here amounts to unveiling the queerness – the supposedly inherent perversity of heterosexual forms of thinking and knowledge – of texts whose authoritative stature is presumably inseparable from their heterosexual structure. Just as in Sullivan's account, queering arguably effects such unveiling by becoming a deconstructive practice projected on to the field of sexuality (Hall 2003: 63).

Finally, in the most recent introduction to date, one might note a partially successful attempt to at least offer new ways of thinking queer theory in the present and the past. Unlike its predecessors, *Queer Theory Now* dedicates a whole chapter to discussing the crucial influence that the AIDS crisis and the new forms of queer activism responding to that crisis had on shaping the concept of queer and queer theory (McCann and Monaghan 2020: 91). It also considers some more current works in queer theory as attempting to go beyond sexuality, identity and antinormativity (2020: 4–5, 14). However, these are compromised and restricted by the same old gesture of confirming queer theory's false problem of definability and its pale solution – the insistence on queer theory's inherent plurality; only this time, the plurality is also manifested in adding to the genealogies of queer theory the influence of LGBT activism and theory (2020: 7). From a Deleuzian critique's perspective, queer's (and queer theory's) problem of definition is as false as the old philosophical problem of the One and the multiple that Deleuze talked about (B 39), if not another iteration of it. Nothing about this problem is singularly queer, but everything about it is a familiar failure to think real difference, which is also to say, multiplicity. No wonder that this introductory book, as it acknowledges the crucial role AIDS played in shaping queer theory, at the same time maintains the separation of queer theory from AIDS discourse in the very chapter that discusses the crisis and queer activism. The authors declare that the chapter 'explores the mechanisms by which AIDS came to influence and act as an "impetus" for queer theory discussion', but in the same paragraph they make a smooth, almost unnoticed shift from AIDS to its analysis (a shift similar to that of Sullivan from queer to queer theory): 'here we seek to expand upon the role of AIDS discourse in shaping queer theory' (McCann and Monaghan 2020: 91).

A Theory to Come

Reflecting back on its moment of emergence, David M. Halperin reminds us in a short essay from 2003 that queer theory, as we know it today, was born as a reaction to an absence of theory, or to an absence *in* Theory, and that it initially functioned as 'a placeholder for a hypothetical knowledge-practice not yet in existence, but whose consummation was devoutly to be wished' (NOR 340). This quote suggests that queer's inherent indeterminacy is not a fact of semantics that simply makes the word 'queer' denote 'strange', 'deceitful' and 'homosexual' in relation to theory, but rather an effect of actual necessity and urgency – a 'set of impossibilities' that necessarily requires and enables the true creation of new possibilities (N 133), which in turn call for an imaginative vision of a different future that might offset the lacuna of the present. Queer theory thus resonated with the compulsory nature of activists' and artists' responses to AIDS that had already been taking place, as seen for example in Bordowitz's description of the formation of AIDS-activist collectives of artists – 'they are leaderless. They function with an extreme sense of urgency' (Bordowitz 2004: 56).

Strangely enough, even though no one knew exactly what queer theory was, says Halperin, 'it became the name of an already established school of theory, as if it constituted a set of specific doctrines' (NOR 340). For Halperin, this façade was an effect of queer theory's swift commodification and institutionalisation, through which it acquired a hegemonic status. In his view, queer theory, despite the challenge it was set to pose to gay and lesbian studies and feminist theory – arguably by deeming them 'under-theorised' and spellbound by identity politics (NOR 341) – was discovered to be exceedingly more prone to institutionalisation than gay and lesbian studies and feminist theory ever were.[7] Halperin is reiterating here an argument he made back in 1995 in *Saint Foucault: Towards A Gay Hagiography*, where he had already identified a disturbing normalising tendency within queer theory, and warned that 'the more it verges on becoming a normative academic discipline, the less queer "queer theory" can plausibly claim to be' (SF 113). Clearly, in the 2003 essay, he considers the normalisation of queer theory already a fait accompli.

Halperin's account of queer theory's normalisation via institutionalisation explains how queer's inherent indeterminacy was compromised once it became a qualifier of 'theory':

The first step was for the 'theory' in queer theory to prevail over 'queer', for 'queer' to be become a harmless qualifier of 'theory': if it's theory ... then ... it can be folded back into the standard practice of literary and cultural studies, without impeding academic business as usual. The next step was to despecify the lesbian, gay, bisexual, transgender, or transgressive content of queerness, thereby abstracting 'queer' and turning it into a generic badge of subversiveness ... if it's queer, it's politically oppositional ... Finally, queer theory ... posed no threat to the monopoly of the established disciplines: on the contrary, queer theory could be incorporated into each of them, and it could then be applied to topics in already established fields. (NOR 341–2)

Halperin's criticism is a clear demonstration of the problem with queer theory's claim to revolutionise thought as such – as if 'queering' equals in principle 'being subversive', or as if a critique of hetero- or homonormativity is revolutionary in itself. Moreover, not only is queer unable to keep theory open and critical, but it also seems to be constrained by a specific sense of 'theory': one that Halperin defines elsewhere, following Foucault, as a set of institutional discursive practices that assert the positivity of their object by determining its truth (HTD 44–5). This type of theoretical practice presupposes the factual nature of both its object and its essential truth, which are believed to be explicable by means of developing 'correct' or 'truthful' means. Every such use of theory, then, implies the founding of a standard for 'correct' application, that is, an independent criterion determining *any* theory's truth value and hence its authority.

Lauren Berlant and Michael Warner advised against such an understanding of queer theory as a systemised worldview endowed with a highly generalising explanatory power of its object – a theory *of* something – precisely because it falsely encourages us, they contend, to 'imagine a context (theory) in which *queer* has a stable referential content and pragmatic force' (Berlant and Warner 1995: 344). While Foucault's *History of Sexuality* challenged the institutional assumption concerning the referential content of sexuality, 'so-called queer theory' (HTD 46), says Halperin, misinterpreted Foucault's critical intervention, and ended up advancing uncritical reproductions of a competing 'truth' by the very same institutional means and in accordance with the same model of truth. Unlike Foucault, queer theory failed to account for the discursive processes that engendered its own truth in the first place.

Halperin's criticism of queer theory betrays a subtle distinction between 'queer' and 'queer theory', suggesting that the relation

Queer Theory's Image of Thought

between the concept and the theory to which it supposedly belongs should at least be problematised. As Foucault defines it in 'The Concern for Truth', problematisation investigates the 'set of discursive or nondiscursive practices that makes something enter into the play of the true and the false, and constitutes it as an object of thought . . .' (FL 456–7). In Halperin's account 'queer theory' is in fact Theory (or High Theory) in disguise – a non-queer, uncritical reproduction of standardised theoretical practices that belong to established academic disciplines. Queer, then, is no longer a concept whose power to unsettle hegemonic theoretical practices is realised by queer theory, but rather a mere 'harmless' qualifier that obscures the fact that there's nothing queer or disturbing about queer theory; it is nothing but Theory by another name (often 'deconstruction'),[8] one that confuses its concept with the truth of its object (conflating queerness with queer subjects or the category of sexuality in general), or its concept's attributes with critical analysis (conflating queerness with theory by qualifying theory itself as strange and disruptive). As we shall see in the next chapter, Halperin's own conceptualisation of queer has nothing to do with its being used as a qualifier of theory, since, for him, queer refers to nothing – it resists being bound to a definitive referent, the truth of which would then be debated or determined by theory. Rather, I think Halperin's concept of queer is best understood as a differential – one that is expressed in the actual differences it engenders (the changing meanings and values it acquires in varying contexts) and determined by its own internal difference. Understanding queer thus explains why Halperin maintains that queer is 'an identity without an essence' or a pure 'positionality' (SF 62) – it is non-referential for it is attached to no identifiable, fixed object; and the only identity it can assume is that of difference, or relation, which is in principle creative (that is, productive), multiplying and ever-changing. For Halperin, queer theory is therefore only pseudo-queer because it relies heavily on a referent: on the presupposed sexual nature of actual subjects and objects (a theory of and about queers) and dominant theoretical practices (what queer theorists call, after Judith Butler, 'the compulsory heterosexual matrix' of culture). Queer theory may very well claim to render its object queer or indeterminate, but the indeterminacy of the object does not guarantee nor substantiate the indeterminacy or plurality (the 'queerness') of theory. On the contrary, by qualifying its object as indeterminate, queer theory becomes all the more referential, and, consequently, determinate and limited in scope, for it presupposes the transcendent, fixed nature of its object – its factual existence beyond doubt or critique. Put differently, queer theory takes sexuality to be the very form of Difference that supposedly precedes and engenders other differences – a move that thus bereaves queer theory's celebrated concept of its differential power as it binds it to an identifiable object.

According to Judith Butler, queer theory's act of methodological founding began with the violent appropriation of sexuality as its own 'proper' object of research. The primary victim of this violence was feminism, which queer theory regarded as a pale theory of gender that is ill-fitted for tackling issues related to sexuality (such as sexual freedom, the formation of sexual identities, the specific problems of sexual minorities and so forth) (Butler 1997: 5, 8–9). Now, while Butler makes a strong case against the 'improper' self-constitution of queer theory at the expense of feminism, her argument implicates an additional consequence – the problem with queer theory is not only the appropriation of its object, but also the *overdetermination* of its concept, that is, the unification and universalisation (a determination 'from above' and 'from without') of the concept of queer that was effected by queer theory's designation of its own proper object of research (its referent). More recently, Butler's critique has been echoed by trans studies for which queer theory is now a privileged institutionalised discourse whose 'universalizing trend' renders anything non-normative its derivative or sub-field, thereby effectively robbing trans studies of the particularity of their issues and methods and of their disciplinary autonomy (Keegan 2020: 351). This problem of queer theory's 'proper' and 'improper' objects (and subjects) has also resurfaced in the writings of scholars working in queer and non-queer theory, who are arguing not just for a subjectless but also objectless queer critique – one that by loosening queer theory's attachment to sexuality opens itself to new paths of critical inquiries that centre on 'the biopolitics of objects', thereby challenging 'human/inhuman assumptions that are prevalent in the field of queer studies' (Eng and Puar 2020: 16). Such projects reinforce this book's argument that queer's true power lies in its affirmation of life in the face of death, a power impelling activists, artists and theorists to conjure up a new mode of existence such as 'chronic life' – a then impossibility that nonetheless made living with (rather than dying from) AIDS a possibility. Such chronic life is now a reality for many (though certainly not all) in Western countries, as AIDS became a liveable condition rather than a death sentence. And of course, such projects are therefore much more akin to Deleuze's non-sexual, vitalist philosophy.

Critique, Abstractions and Universals

Halperin's critique of queer theory suggests a distinction between the concept of queer and the practice of queer theory. But how could queer theory be said to have no hold over its own principal concept? Has queer theory not been faithful enough to the differential definition of queer by insisting on its indeterminacy and by refusing any ultimate definition? Moreover, has the discussion so far not amounted to privileging one definition of queer over others, and consequently risking establishing the truth of the concept while at the same time arguing against theoretical practices, which similarly establish the truth of their own analytical procedures and their objects? The key to understanding the implications and scope of the distinction between queer as a concept and queer as a qualifier of theory, as well as to forming an adequate response to such charges, is to clarify under what conditions queer functions as a critical concept. Adapting the procedure that I described earlier as Deleuzian critique to this task, and following Iain MacKenzie's argument that Deleuze and Guattari's definition of philosophy as constructivism 'culminates in a carefully crafted account of what it is to be a social critic', and that their last collaborative book *What is Philosophy?* 'is the most convincing attempt to date to reveal the philosophical claims implicit within post-structuralist theoretical analysis and critical practice' (1997: 7), I argue that queer functions critically inasmuch as it is constructed philosophically. Through a close reading of Halperin's *Saint Foucault* alongside Deleuze and Guattari's *What is Philosophy?* I show in the next chapter how a philosophical concept of queer can be constructed anew in and through Halperin's work.

To this end, we must first rid ourselves of the false problem of the plurality of queer theory, for we gain no useful knowledge of queer when we are presented with a hodgepodge of definitions taken from different texts and contexts that testifies to the concept's being a genuine multiplicity. This strategy, which is often employed by introductions to queer theory as we saw in the previous section, supposedly demonstrates the concept's inherent indeterminacy, functional elasticity and resistance to exclusive definition or meaning. Treated by constructivism, however, the concept of queer seems no more indeterminate or multiple than any other concept; and if its supposed essential indeterminacy holds any critical and practical value, it cannot be grounded on the quantifiable diversity of its actualisations, but rather on its internal difference that determines its potentiality or power. Otherwise, even a concept such as sexual difference – a concept that, according to Butler, queer theory was compelled to distort and reduce to assign it to a degenerate feminism, so that queer theory could then reclaim it under a supposedly more critical and advanced concept such as sexuality (1997: 4–9) – might easily be considered to offer the very same indeterminacy as its own critical advantage.

This is precisely the point that Elizabeth Grosz persuasively makes when she accounts for how feminist theory makes a difference. Following Deleuze and Guattari, she defines feminist theory as a philosophical practice of creating concepts, and the concept of sexual difference as an ever-changing multiplicity that mobilises the whole field of feminist thought towards new ways of thinking, even beyond itself:

> Feminist philosophy is the positing of sexual difference not as an answer or solution, but as the question that has not been adequately framed and addressed until very recently and that is the frame from which many other, possibly infinite, questions can be directed to other disciplines, knowledges, and forms of practice. The very commitment to sexual difference or gender equality already entails a kind of philosophy, a conceptual understanding of what it is that feminism itself must be in order to be political. (Grosz 2010: 102)

In her reading, it is in fact feminism's continuous problematisation of the concept of sexual difference that has enriched, transformed and invigorated the mid-twentieth-century philosophical conceptualisation of 'difference in-itself' or 'pure difference', enabling philosophy to multiply differences and address new audiences and the specificities of their lived experience (Grosz 2010: 103–5). The concept of sexual difference is a powerful means to rethink the present and to effect political change, Grosz argues, for it is 'the virtual force that enables another perspective, position, or body than that which is socially dominant to be revealed in the operations of that domination' (2010: 105). If we consider both Butler's critique of queer theory and Grosz's account of the difference feminism makes, it seems unlikely to presume that queer's indeterminacy holds a superior critical advantage, if such presumption merely comes down to displacing the concept of sexual difference and incorporating it into a more 'proper' concept such as sexuality. If we are to understand how queer can function as a concept affirming difference, thereby endowing thought with new means and critical edge, and how it can relate to new and different contexts and problems, as well as to other concepts of other theoretical practices and disciplines, it may prove more beneficial to consider that indeterminacy is not a privileged property of the concept of queer, and to inquire what queer as a concept can do – what difference does it make, or how to account for the singularity of its construction.

Determining the problems to which the concept serves as a solution is key to understanding the critical and practical nature of constructing concepts as well as to evaluating the concept itself. Let us first consider the question of value. Deleuze and Guattari argue that, in fact, without the simultaneous construction of the problems to which the concept relates, it is impossible to determine the value of any concept. Their first example is the famous Cartesian *cogito*, a concept of the self – is it a good or a bad concept? Can we determine its value without already changing the problem? They reply:

> There is no point in wondering whether Descartes was right or wrong... Can thought as such be the verb of an I? There is no direct answer. Cartesian concepts can only be assessed as a function of their problems and their plane... concepts can only be replaced by others if there are new problems and another plane relative to which (for example) 'I' loses all meaning, the beginning [the subjective presupposition of the I that doubts everything but cannot doubt its own thinking and being] loses all necessity, and the presuppositions [subjective or objective] lose all difference – or take no other... Is there one plane that is better than all others, or problems that dominate all others? Nothing can be said at this point. Planes must be constructed and problems posed, just as concepts must be created... If one concept is 'better' than an earlier one, it is because it makes us aware of new variations and unknown resonances, it carries out unforeseen cuttings-out, it brings forth an Event that surveys us. (WP 27–8)

To criticise a concept, then, necessarily means to evaluate that concept by reconstructing or changing it in relation to a new problem. As Deleuze and Guattari show, this is exactly what Kant did when he criticised Descartes for overlooking or misconceiving the temporal form under which the I that thinks determines its own being (WP 31–2). Daniel Smith explains: 'To say that Kant "criticised" Descartes is simply to say that Kant constructed a problem that could not be occupied or completed by the Cartesian *cogito*' (2012: 135).

The temporal form of the I becomes in Kant's critique the new problem in relation to which the concept of the *cogito* is reconstructed so as to be complemented with a new component, namely, 'time', which is itself a new concept created by Kant and which can no longer be understood solely in terms of succession, as Descartes thought of it: 'If Kant introduced time as a new component of the cogito, he did so on the condition of creating a new concept of time: time now becomes a form of interiority with its own internal components (succession, but also simultaneity and permanence)' (Smith 2012: 135).

What I refer to here as 'abstraction' is the outcome of a failure to relate queer to a problem. Abstractions of queer provide no measure for determining whether queer is a good or a bad concept for two reasons: they exclude the problems in relation to which queer was formed in different contexts as a solution; and they fail to construct a new problem in relation to which queer, even in the form of a mélange of definitions, is a solution. Disregarding the problem to which an idea or concept corresponds results in a failed critique, as can be clearly seen in Deleuze's comment on negative interpretative readings of Foucault: 'They're not readings at all and are quite irrelevant; they come down to criticizing vague ideas of things Foucault said, without taking any account whatever of the problems to which they relate' (N 84).

The strategy of grouping together different definitions of queer to demonstrate its plural, hence indeterminate, nature – which is usually followed by pinpointing their common features to impose on the concept a semblance and a generality that will enable it to be communicated – is a form of such an abstraction. Abstractions such as this are symptoms of false problems – definitions of queer are severed from their respective problems and contexts in order to endow queer, however reluctantly, with a faint stability – and I dare say, identity – that is presumed to be essential if we are to be able to employ such an indeterminate, evasive concept. In Todd May's discussion of Deleuze's philosophy of difference, he argues that conceptual stability is a requirement only for an 'ontology of discovery' that presupposes the nature and essence of the objects it investigates. Such an ontology limits itself to discovering 'what is' – the self-identity of existing entities – and thus requires conceptual stability to identify the fixed, unchanging characteristics of its objects. May argues that Deleuze's 'creative ontology', however, refuses to subject difference and change to identity, and instead sees difference, flux and change as the essence of being. Such an ontology replaces conceptual stability with differential concepts that have nothing to do with discovery: 'a concept is a way of addressing the difference that lies beneath the identities we experience' (May 2005: 19).

But what is wrong with abstractions of queer and its formulation as a universal? This is where the critical nature of constructing concepts becomes a pivotal factor of evaluation. Each time the problems queer is set to 'solve' are cancelled out in abstractions, the concept's critical edge becomes drastically obtuse. For Halperin, once queer qualifies theory it becomes an empty, abstract label of subversiveness that merely allows the concept (and queer theory) to be tolerated by and incorporated into hegemonic, normalising, 'serious' disciplines and theoretical practices – the very same heteronormative institutions that queer was designed to undermine (NOR 341). For Butler, when we use queer as an ultimate concept, supposedly radical in itself and hence implicitly superior to other concepts, we remain forever entangled in and subjected to the political interplay of exclusion and inclusion that characterises identity politics, against which the challenge of queer politics had been set from the start (1993: 230). Grosz's account of sexual difference as a concept, although not contrived as part of an outspoken charge against queer, demonstrates the fundamental openness of feminist theory's most debated concept, its practical and political usefulness, and its formative role in shaping contemporary feminist and philosophical thought. In comparison, queer does not seem to offer anything radical and new that is not already subsumed in sexual difference.

Above all, these criticisms point towards an idea of critique against which queer's lack of critical edge as a concept can be assessed. A legacy of the project of the Enlightenment and particularly of Kant's philosophy, the idea of critique, argues Iain MacKenzie, is designed as a reaction to indifferentism, which is the effect and the sign of a pointless, exhausted form of metaphysics, represented by two rival approaches – dogmatism and scepticism – both of which are described by Kant as popular philosophies that are not as oppositional as they believe themselves to be, for they share the same image of thought: a thought that can only engage in a pointless debate between claim and counter-claim without ever subjecting its own presuppositions to the test of critique; a superficial thought that constitutes itself as the true thinking of reason yet fails to construct a concept of reason, its powers and its limits. Kant's idea of critique was set against the indifference to metaphysical presuppositions effected by popular debates devoid of philosophical substance.

But, MacKenzie goes on, Kant saw critique also as a forceful and necessary means to overcome indifference manifested in the dangerously lazy, immature, habitual ways of thinking of the public in his times, the 'naïve and uncritical obedience to those who order our public life and control our private beliefs' (2004: 3). For Kant, says MacKenzie, indifference to philosophical problems and social apathy are intimately related, and only critique can bring them into relief: 'the need for an idea of critique adequate to the task of meeting and confounding indifference, therefore, is also the need for a reflective and mature civil society upon which to found enlightened apparatuses of government' (2004: 4). Kant set two criteria to which critique must adhere if it is to overcome indifference: totality and immanence. Critique is total in the sense that nothing escapes it, not even its own presuppositions and methodological procedures; it is immanent in the sense that it is neither conditioned by nor subjected to anything outside itself. It is never immanent *to* something else, only to itself. If there was some transcendent instance, value or organising principle beyond its reach, total critique would be impossible or become partial at best.

Queer, constructed either as a qualifier (in the case of queer theory) or an abstraction (in the case of introductions), fails to fulfil these two criteria because in both cases it is made referential. As a qualifier of theory, queer loses all indeterminacy by qualifying theoretical practice and simultaneously intensifying its sexual sense, so that queer now refers either to actual subjects (queers); or to the proper object of theory (sexuality); or to the indeterminate and thus presumably subversive operations of theory (queering, which is itself often considered to be referring to deconstruction); or to the ideal quality that bequeaths a common (that is, mutual and conventional) sense (queerness) to all referents. Queer theory, then, can only amount to what MacKenzie describes as 'partial criticism': neither total nor immanent, partial criticism criticises only part of an idea, but remains partial to the idea as a meaningful, undebatable whole, so that the idea is safely placed beyond the reach of criticism (2004: 22–7). This is exactly what queer theory becomes, when, according to Butler, it illegitimately appropriates sexuality as its proper object of research as it adopts a confused, uncritical view of the categories of sex and gender and the complex ways in which they inform sexuality. Queer theory's idea of sexuality – though reconstructed anew as fluid, indeterminate, multiple and non-binary – excludes a critical account of the procedures (the divisions, distinctions, allocations) involved in its construction, such as the conflation of sex with gender, and the reformulation of a concept of sex that denies the commonality of interest in it shared by both feminism and queer theory (Butler 1997: 4–5).

The charge against queer theory's partiality to the idea of sexuality is also evident once we relate Halperin's argument about queer theory's misinterpretation of Foucault to the distinction he draws between a liberal and a queer concept of freedom. As a normalising practice, queer theory can only advocate a sexual politics that is bound to a liberal concept of freedom, that is, 'a regulative or normative ideal of responsible and self-respecting human conduct' (SF 21). This brand of sexual politics only affirms and bolsters the very power structures its goal was to overthrow, because it embraces the sense of freedom advocated and imposed by the modern regime of sexuality. Consequently, queer theory can be rightly argued to be oblivious to what Halperin considers as Foucault's important lesson: 'sexual liberation may have liberated our sexuality but it has not liberated us *from* our sexuality; if anything, it has enslaved us more profoundly to it' (SF 20). As long as queer theory refrains from subjecting the idea of sexuality to the scrutiny of critique – reconstructing it immanently in relation to problems, and accounting for its powers and limits even at the price of its total destruction – it can offer nothing but the same, self-defeating version of liberal sexual politics, or amount to a partial criticism that multiplies and disseminates the same hegemonic (heteronormative) idea of sexuality that it criticises.

Abstractions of queer are no less referential and thus no more immanent and total than queer as a qualifier of theory. In abstractions, queer becomes a universal, or an 'ultimate concept' (WP 15) – a fixed, transcendent reference point that is called upon to criticise something without ever being itself the subject of such criticism. Universalism allows us to identify queerness wherever it appears and reappears, whether in lived experience or in the theoretical procedures of queer theory. Queer, therefore, always remains the same, or its radical difference (its indeterminacy) is revealed to be compromised and secondary, for it is deduced from or reduced to a universal Queerness the actualisations of which all resemble each other as well as their 'originating' abstract quality. An abstraction of queer can generally be said to follow what I term 'the Universal theorem': the queer (q) concept (c) minus the problems to which it relates ($p_{1,2,3...n}$), plus a dimension of emptiness that marks the absence of a new problem (0), so that: $c - p_n + 0$. This theorem cannot be equated with the construction of the concept but with the assumption of Queerness (Q) as a

Universal (U), so that: $U(Q) = c - p_n + 0$. When the concept turns into a universal, it renders its internal difference secondary and derivative in relation to its presupposed fixed identity – a Queerness identified in and referred to its actualisations. Ironically, the infamous, so-called postmodern concept reveals itself to be akin more to the Platonic Idea than to any postmodern concept of difference once it is sexually overdetermined (unified, determined 'from above') by its own indeterminacy. As a universal, queer always refers back to its ideal, transcendent form, which in turn enables the identification of queer in its actualisations by means of analogy and representation ('queering' is *like* 'deconstruction'; 'queer' *stands for* 'subversiveness'); and also the subsumption of all that is queer in a transcendent idea of Queerness. This is how queer as an abstraction fails to meet the criteria of critique: it becomes immanent *to* something else (an ideal quality) and not to itself; and its ideal, transcendent form as a universal remains forever beyond the reach of critique, thereby precluding total critique.[9]

Universals can never be tools of critique, Deleuze and Guattari argue, for they 'explain nothing but must themselves be explained' (WP 7). Early on they define universals as the products of three conceptions of philosophy that they replace with the notion of constructivism: contemplation, reflection and communication. MacKenzie describes these three conceptions of philosophy through the transformation of the Idea. Contemplation (or objective idealism) is the branch of philosophy that presupposes the existence of a transcendent object (the Platonic Idea) against which all its actualisations can be evaluated. Reflection (or subjective idealism) is the branch of philosophy that renders the transcendent Idea immanent to the thinking subject (as in Descartes's and Kant's versions of the *cogito*), thereby altering the sense of objectivity: 'objectivity here will assume a certainty of knowledge rather than presuppose a truth recognised as pre-existing, or already there' (WP 27). Communication (or intersubjective idealism) effects another transformation of the Idea: the transcendental subject (as it was formed by the Kantian take on subjective idealism) is now empirically grounded on experience (as in Husserl's phenomenology), and therefore the Idea becomes the consequence of the communication between either intentional objects, other selves (subjects), or culture and community. In all three branches of philosophy, the Idea 'becomes a transcendent universal, and the plane becomes an attribute in the concept' (WP 44–5); that is, the concept is confused with the plane.

Queer Theory's Image of Thought

Against its false universality, queer can function as a critical concept only on condition that it becomes a philosophical concept that is the product of constructivism. For this reason I would argue that queer is a rare concept and that queer theory in most cases amounts to partial criticism. Halperin's *Saint Foucault* is one of the rare occasions on which queer was carefully constructed as a concept, and this text will be the focus of the next chapter.[10] I would argue, then, that Halperin's *Saint Foucault* is not strictly a work of queer theory, but rather a form of constructivism – or a theoretical 'hagiography' of sorts, if we take its subtitle seriously – in which queer functions as the critical instance that brings the truth of other concepts (such as power, politics, identity, subjectivity, desire, sexuality) into crisis. What critics of queer theory overlook when they refer to Halperin's conceptualisation of queer or cite it out of context is that he practises exactly what he preaches: he does not use the concept of queer as a universal but as a differential concept; he does not give us a unified, fixed definition of queer that can be simply repeated or reapplied in other contexts without undergoing a qualitative change, and without effecting further differences. Instead, I argue, Halperin created *a* concept of queer that is both consistent and infinitely variable; one that is inseparable from the actual circumstances under which it emerged (the contingency of AIDS as event) yet is unexhausted by them. The merit of such an argument will become clearer if we reconstruct queer as a philosophical concept in a reading of Halperin's work, identify the problems it was set to solve, and account for the value of the concept for our present problems.

However, reconstructing the concept does not mean simply describing it as if it is already given, not least because my employment of Deleuzian critique does not always make clear differentiations between Halperin's, Foucault's and my own voice. The queer concept is constructed here anew, since it also comes to bear on problems and concepts that Halperin did not necessarily address. In this sense, I take Deleuze and Guattari's view of philosophy as the creation of concepts very practically: the concept must be created even if it is an old concept, and even if it bears the same name and belongs to the work of another thinker. In this sense, I am critical of Halperin as much as I admire his work. But I criticise Halperin only in a specific sense:

> to criticize is only to establish that a concept vanishes when it is thrust into a new milieu, losing some of its components, or acquiring others

that transform it. But those who criticize without creating, those who are content to defend the vanished concept without being able to give it the forces it needs to return to life, are the plague of philosophy. (WP 28)

By connecting Halperin's concept of queer to a new milieu – which includes not only the thought of Deleuze and Guattari but also the concerns of our present – I am hoping to create a philosophical concept of queer that appears as fresh and new and strange as it once was.

This attempt will be manifested in a detailed discussion of all three activities of constructivism that do not appear as such (or at all) in Halperin. For example, Halperin only scarcely and haphazardly mentions Foucault's alleged saintliness, but in my account Foucault becomes a full-fledged conceptual persona that I dub 'the exemplary saint'. Similarly, although Halperin scarcely alludes to the question of freedom, in my account freedom forms the conditions of queer's thinkability as a concept. And while I believe Halperin would not object to my argument that his often cited definition of queer accounts for only part of the concept as he conceived of it, the relation between what I will call in the next chapter 'the two points of view' that are constitutive of queer is not given as such in the text (nor are the concept's components as I describe them). And, as I shall argue in Chapter 3, this relation between the two points of view entails further problems (such as the problem of thinking the relation between queer thought and queer practices) that must be addressed if we are to put the concept to practical use today. Nevertheless, just as Halperin lets his attentive reading of Foucault shape his concept of queer, I endeavour to offer a reading of both Halperin and Foucault, but also of and alongside Deleuze and Guattari, which is as attentive as it is enabling and creative.

Notes

1. The Oxford English Dictionary also notes that this 'strangeness' itself functioned negatively early on, denoting something suspicious, contemptible and worthless, even before it was used as a derogatory term for homosexuals.
2. See, for example, Jagose 2015, and all the essays in this special issue of *differences*, entitled 'Queer Theory without Antinormativity'.
3. For a different sense of 'after queer theory', see Hoad 2007: 517; Halley and Parker 2011.
4. For a counter criticism of Jeffreys, see Hall 2003: 83.

5. A recent study offers a different take on this problem in queer anthropology, although I think it clearly applies to the use of queer theory in general regardless of discipline. See Weiss 2022.
6. Sullivan retains throughout her book this sense of queer as 'queer theory', which operates by deconstructing any actual manifestation of heteronormativity, and so renders the identification (hence fixation) of queer theory or 'queering' always possible in principle. Consequently, queering popular culture, for instance, comes to mean uncovering (or what I consider recovering) 'the (repressed) homosexual or homoerotic elements ... contained in mainstream cinematic texts' (Sullivan 2003: 192). Here heteronormativity is even more literal, and the process of queering ever more attached to the object it rediscovers in texts. Then, when queering results in uncovering a 'gay sensibility' within texts (2003: 193), Sullivan relates it to the concept of 'camp', which ends up being reincorporated into the practice of queer theory; that is, 'camp' is said to be describing 'the ways in which particular texts, or elements thereof, queer – in the broadest sense of the term – heteronormative values, beliefs, and institutions' (2003: 194).
7. Halperin does not explain here why this rapid institutionalisation took place. For a materialist account of queer theory's institutionalisation in the broader framework of the history of sexuality studies, see Penney 2014: 71–80.
8. For an elaborate and critical discussion of queer theory as a deconstructive practice, see Seidman 1995.
9. For Deleuze and Guatarri's account of how universals make immanence 'immanent to', see WP 44–50.
10. Regarding the rarity of queer as a concept, I do not mean to suggest that such a critical concept can be found only in Halperin. Lee Edelman's *No Future* (2004), for example, can be seen as another intricate example of a meticulously constructed concept of queer. Michael Warner and Judith Butler provide compelling definitions of queer, particularly in relation to its critical and political value, but I think that they use it more as a guideline than a concept. In Butler's case, the dominant concept in her work is obviously performativity, and I think it is not coincidental that queer is absent from *Gender Trouble* and appears only later in *Bodies that Matter* as part of her clarifications of the concept of performativity. What I find problematic in the context of my discussion here is the recurrent tendency within queer theory not only to consider *Gender Trouble* as its founding text, but also to equate queer with performativity, rather than accounting for how queer informs and relates to the specific problems that Butler addresses.

2

Philosophically Queer: Constructing a Concept

In *Saint Foucault: Towards a Gay Hagiography*, David Halperin famously defines 'queer' as 'an identity without an essence', an imposed discursive marginal location that is 'by definition *whatever* is at odds with the normal, the legitimate, the dominant' (SF 62). For too long this enticing, oft-cited definition has functioned uncritically as queer theorists' shaky conceptual ground. Conversely, the ungrounding procedure of Deleuzian critique renders the question of the concept's legitimate use inseparable from deducing the problem to which queer serves as a solution. Thus, in its trajectory towards the virtual sphere of problems, critique's point of departure would be the determination of the author's actual problem, stated either explicitly or implicitly. In a strategic use of the first-person pronoun (whose function will become clearer in the following discussion), Halperin puts forth the problem of authority as that which the constructivist method I offer deduces as the condition for the queer solution:

> How, as a gay man, an academic, and a public intellectual, I can acquire and maintain the authority to speak, to be heard, and to be taken seriously without denying or bracketing my gayness. It's not just a matter of being publicly or visibly out; it's a matter of being able to devise and to preserve a positive, undemonized connection between my gayness and my scholarly or critical authority. (SF 8)

For Halperin, authority reappeared historically in a new, problematic form: not the denial of the right to speak and be heard from which sexual minorities have suffered – to an extent, this problem was 'solved' in the aftermath of the Stonewall Riots of 1969 – but rather the denial of any claim to knowledge to people of non-normative sexual identity.[1]

The actual event that both expressed the problem of authoritative knowledge in this form and made it an urgent one was the AIDS crisis in the United States, which engendered a new form of activism that insisted, according to Halperin, on the irreducibly sexual nature of the problem and therefore on the necessity of new strategies of response: 'in order to be effective, AIDS activism has had to challenge traditional modes of empowering knowledge as well as traditional modes of authorizing and legitimating power' (SF 28). AIDS became a problem for sexual politics, particularly for gay politics, because in the first years of its course it was dubbed 'a gay disease'; and before the CDC (American Center for Disease Control) officially named it 'AIDS' – Acquired Immunodeficiency Syndrome – in 1982, medical professionals and researchers named it 'GRID' – Gay Related Immune Deficiency.[2] Not only did AIDS kill at a frighteningly accelerating rate, but it also evolved into a full-fledged cultural crisis manifested in multiple social and political arenas. Early on, critical accounts of AIDS considered it more than just a disease whose effects and significance were determined solely by the dry facts of science. Rather, AIDS was described, for example, as a medical condition whose supposedly factual, scientific definition was grounded on metaphors that disseminated conceptions of the disease as an attack on the social body, and that assigned blame to the disease's 'sexually deviant' victims (Sontag 1989); as an 'epidemic of signification', a 'nexus where multiple meanings, stories, and discourses intersect and overlap, reinforce and subvert each other' (Treichler 1999: 19), thereby revealing the prior, socially constructed basis of the biomedical discourse that 'made sense' of the disease; and as a crisis of representation that threatened the very existence of the gay way of life (Watney 1997: 9). Such critical analyses of the processes generating the meanings of AIDS in multiple discourses reveal that what we have come to know as the reality of AIDS – the 'truth' of its existence – has been shaped by social forces that traverse and condition both the disciplines determining the 'objective' nature of the disease and the lived experience of the individuals and groups affected by it. AIDS marked a historical critical point where the forces constituting authoritative knowledge – from the conventional linguistic means of sense-making, to the genealogies of metaphors of illness, to the history and structure of 'narratives of contagion' (Wald 2008) – became visible through their political and cultural effects.

These effects – ranging from the Reagan administration's negligent indifference towards AIDS, to the varying degrees of violence inflicted mainly upon gay men – led scholars and activists to uncover and debate the homophobic nature of the underlying logic of authoritative knowledge in the age of AIDS. In Halperin's view, the shift in gay politics from a model of liberation (focused primarily on reforming official policies and laws) to a model of resistance and survival (such as the ACT UP movement's model that was based on direct action and civil disobedience)[3] is related to (if not derived from) the influence of the Foucauldian analytics of power in the first volume of *The History of Sexuality* as a diffuse network of relations between forces acting on one another. These power-relations traverse the entire social field and are inseparable from (though not identical to) the formation of knowledge and truth of a particular historical age:

> it has become increasingly clear to gay men in the United States that what we are up against . . . is not only . . . specific agents of oppression, such as gay-bashers or the police, nor formal, explicit interdictions . . . nor even particular, hostile institutions . . . but rather pervasive, multiform strategies of homophobia that shape public and private discourses. (SF 32)[4]

Homophobia, argues Halperin, is not an isolated social phenomenon, nor can it be reduced to a specific content that can be dismissed by rational explanations; rather, it functions 'as part of more general and systemic strategies of delegitimation' (SF 32).

Homophobic discourses are strategically and inherently incoherent, for they operate by means of logical contradictions that enable them to disempower gays and lesbians by delegitimising their ways of life and self-knowing. His prime example is Sedgwick's analysis of the epistemology of the closet, where the closet is a figure of an impasse that reveals the futility of any attempt either to 'remain in' or 'come out' – it will always be deemed too early or too late, yet the effect of coming out in either case will nonetheless be damaging. As long as the description of coming out is susceptible to discursive logical contradictions (such as something that is both too early and already too late), there is no way to win 'the homophobic game of truth' (SF 38), and coming out will not prove itself to be an effective tool for fighting prejudice.

In other words, there is no point in struggling over the truth of sexuality, if sexuality itself functions as both the ground and object of knowledge for a discursive practice. Discourses of sexuality draw their authority not from neutral, scientific or speculative procedures, but rather from a privileged heterosexual position of power disguised as a universal, unbiased way of knowing. Homosexuality thus becomes an object of critical examination denuded of any content of its own, for it is defined only negatively as that which deviates from normative, 'right' or 'true' (hetero)sexuality:

> heterosexuality itself is never an *object* of knowledge . . . so much as it is a *condition* for the supposedly objective, disinterested knowledge of *other*

objects, especially homosexuality, which it constantly produces as a ... contradictory figure of transgression so as to deflect attention – by means of accusation – from its own incoherence. (SF 47)

As Halperin himself notes, this insight, which led to critiques of heterosexuality and analyses of homophobic discursive strategies, later constituted the main objectives and 'grounding axioms' of what came to be known in the 1990s as queer theory (SF 47).

What some activists and scholars realised early on was that AIDS cannot be fought at the level of truth or knowledge alone – it is never simply a matter of telling or knowing the truth of either AIDS, sexuality or their supposed interrelation; rather, AIDS should be fought at the level of power, or perhaps more accurately, at the level of what Foucault called power/knowledge. If the AIDS crisis was overdetermined by the homophobic discourses that produced scientific knowledge, cultural representations and official policies, then the relation between Halperin's initial positing of the problem of authority as personal and the collective nature of its rephrased formulation becomes conspicuous: 'what opportunities does the discursive formation of sexuality create for discursive counterpractices? What sort of antihomophobic strategies does the apparatus of homophobia make possible?' (SF 48). Halperin recounts several responses to this challenge, all of which lay bare the strategies of homophobic discourses that underlie the discourses of law, science, medicine and religion in order to 'find ways of frustrating the political strategies immanent in their deployment, of delegitimizing their claims to authority and dismantling their institutional base' (SF 52).

But Halperin's concept of queer does not respond to this problem in the same way, since it follows Foucault's 'different tactic' – one that entails a further elaboration of the problem in terms of resisting authoritative power/knowledge apparatuses. When he describes Foucault's political involvement with *Groupe d'information sur les prisons* (the Prison Information Group that Foucault founded with Jean-Marie Domenach and Pierre Vidal-Naquet in 1971), Halperin explains that Foucault and the group's aim was not liberation, but resistance; not speaking on behalf of the oppressed and proposing reforms to institutions (that is, regaining access to institutional power as in the liberationist model of participatory democracy), but rather creating and multiplying the conditions under which the disempowered can speak for themselves, by strategically altering the positions of both oppressors and oppressed:

'his [Foucault's] efforts were directed to *resisting* specific forms of social domination effected and legitimized by specific apparatuses of power/knowledge, and his characteristic tactic was to attempt to reverse the subject- and object-positions typically assigned by those apparatuses to the empowered and disempowered, respectively' (SF 56, my emphasis). Halperin then offers a brief genealogy of gay and lesbian anti-authoritarian struggles, and further distinguishes between them in terms of their strategy to effect a 'discursive reversal', or an attempt to resist authority by way of shifting the disempowered homosexual from the position of the object to that of the subject.

Only then does his concept of queer emerge as a distinctive solution to the problem of authoritative power/knowledge – a response that differs in kind from the past oppositional reactions of the Homophile movements and the Gay Liberation movements. From the perspective of Deleuzian critique, the AIDS crisis comes to mark the contingency or event that determines both the conditions of the problem and the possibilities for oppositional activist response (that is, cases of solution), and thus we can now reformulate the problem of authority in the following way: *how does one resist preponderant forms of authority that reduce one to an object of knowledge and at the same time deny one the position of a knowing subject?* Before Halperin provides his famous and widely cited definition of queer in its difference from gay, he neatly summarises the difference of the queer discursive reversal: queer resists by 'assuming' or 'taking advantage of' the empty, purely negative, oppositional position that homophobic discourses had imposed on homosexuals, in order to create new identities that lack any definitional content: 'those who knowingly occupy such a marginal location, who assume a de-essentialized identity that is purely positional in character, are properly speaking not gay but *queer*' (SF 62).

I argue that when Halperin finally defines queer – as that which refers to nothing in particular and therefore as that whose actual and constantly shifting content is a function of the oppositional relation that queer forms with the normative – we should bear in mind that he is in fact telling us 1) under what *conditions* queer can be said to resist; and, consequently, 2) that queer resistance is actualised as a shift from the object-position to the subject-position, which together with the shift itself are all immanent to a historically determined formation of power-relations. Therefore, all we can say at this point is that by reversing or shifting the position of the object to that of the subject, queer constitutes a solution to the problem of authority as it was reformulated above.

Thus far, Halperin says nothing about *how* or *by what means* resistance will be actualised either discursively or non-discursively; and he most definitely does not imply that simply 'being' queer miraculously makes one politically subversive in any way. In fact, we might recall that in his critique of queer theory – which in *Saint Foucault* appears as a warning and in later texts as queer theory's overly exhausted limit – queer does not mark resistance at all, but rather has become 'an empty label of subversiveness' denuded of any content. Criticisms of queer theory's insistence on queer's non-specificity and indeterminacy – such as Alan McKee's, who argued that 'in the face of a resolved and insistent unknowablity [sic], it remains clear that Queer *means*' and that '"Queer" is not an entirely empty signifier' (1999: 237) – are misguided, particularly in Halperin's case. Queer is non-referential *because* it resists, and not the other way around; non-referentiality is not something the concept has to possess in order to resist; on the contrary – it is already a function and effect of an act of resistance that had occurred immanently within a given formation of power-relations. Queer is indeterminate or lacking fixed content not because the concept is non-referential; rather, queer is indeterminate because the actual, particular content it will have assumed is dependent on and derived from its virtual oppositional relation to the normative within a given formation of power-relations. Therefore, queer is a concept of resistance in two complementary senses: 1) what Halperin dubs a 'positionality', that is, an ideal or virtual shift within power-relations that marks their transformation. As such, it constitutes the limit of a given formation of power-relations or its potential of change. 2) It is a position, that is, an actualised instance of such movement whereby one shifts from the object-position to the subject-position. We can find in Halperin an account for both senses, but his widely cited definition of queer accounts only for the first one. This explains why attempts to ground 'queering' on Halperin's definition of queer, which neither relate the concept to the problem it was set to solve nor construct a new problem upon which it is conditioned as a solution, become sorely uncritical: they privilege an abstraction of the first sense while disregarding the second.

In fact, the elaboration of queer's second sense, or *how* queer is said to resist, can be found in the second half of Halperin's book's second chapter. Simply put, queer resists (or shifts from the position of the object to that of the subject) by becoming other than itself. More to the point, queer resists *by cultivating an impersonal self, that is, by activating a reflexive relation of the self to itself that strategically seeks after that which transcends itself.* In other words, one resists queerly by taking up an imposed, underprivileged position to become other than what one currently is. Queer resists in the sense that it enters a becoming-other – it transforms and recreates its self by relating to itself, thereby shifting from the position of object to that of subject. The key to understanding this second sense of queer, and thus the queer solution in its entirety, lies in the way Halperin links two phases in Foucault's work, sometimes referred to as the 'middle Foucault' and the 'late Foucault', or his conception of politics with his conception of ethics. I would even venture to say that *Saint Foucault* can be seen in its entirety as a profound *explication de texte* focused on Foucault's controversial argument in the first volume of *The History of Sexuality*, 'where there is power, there is resistance' (HV1 95), except that Halperin explains this claim by incorporating Foucault's later work on the care of the self as an ethical practice (particularly as it is discussed in the second and third volumes of *The History of Sexuality*, and in the series of lectures at the Collège de France), and Foucault's own critique of gay politics, where his conception of ancient ethics is clearly present.

With the elaboration of the ethical (second) sense of queer, Halperin expands his preliminary observation about the emergence of a new model of gay politics, one that is based on resistance rather than liberation. Queer resistance is not simply the negation of the normative, but also a creative practice of freedom whereby new identities are created within given power-relations. Halperin suggests considering this creative act as what Foucault called 'ethics' or the 'aesthetics of existence' – the ancient Greek and Roman practices of self-fashioning. Foucault discovered the technology for such self-transformation in the Ancient Greek ἄσκησις (*askēsis*) or 'ascetics': a spiritual exercise or self-stylisation that enables one to transform oneself, and render one's existence distinct, beautiful and powerful.[5] Foucault defines *askēsis* as 'an exercise of self upon self by which one tries to work out, to transform one's self and to attain a certain mode of being' (E 282). Such a practice founds a strategic relation to oneself, a cultivation of the self through various ascetic practices (which vary from one philosophical school to another);[6] but, crucially, Halperin emphasises that the self that is being cultivated is not a personal identity nor a psychological dimension of depth, but an impersonal self that transcends the individual:

> Hence, to cultivate oneself . . . is not to explore or experience some given self . . . but instead to use one's relation to oneself as a potential resource with which to construct new modalities of subjective agency and new styles of personal life that may enable one to resist or even to escape one's social and psychological determinations. To practice a stylistics of the self ultimately means to cultivate that part of oneself that leads beyond oneself . . . it is to elaborate the strategic possibilities of what is the most *impersonal* dimension of personal life – namely, the capacity to 'realize oneself' by becoming other than what one is. (SF 76)

The impersonal self to be cultivated is a form of radical otherness, and the practice of the care of the self effects self-transformation through which one becomes other than oneself. In Antiquity, the soul was believed to be a particle of the divine, and cultivating an impersonal self therefore meant actualising a divine moral quality, such as σωφροσύνη (*sophrosynē*) – self-restraint or moderation. Foucault sees such a practice as ethical in nature, but he gives ethics a broader sense based on the Greek meaning of *ēthos*:

> *ēthos* was a way of being and of behavior. It was a mode of being for the subject, along with a certain way of acting, a way visible to others . . . For the Greeks, this was the concrete form of freedom . . . A man possessed of a splendid *ēthos* . . . was someone who practiced freedom in a certain way . . . But extensive work by the self on the self is required for this practice of freedom to take shape in an *ēthos* that is good, beautiful, honorable, estimable, memorable, and exemplary. (E 286)[7]

Halperin explains that Foucault considered not only philosophy but also homosexuality as a modern art of life through which subjects might transform their existence. This is the self-transforming ethical practice, or what Foucault identified as the task of becoming homosexual, which Halperin rewrites as queer: 'his [Foucault's] remarks make sense only if he understood his term "homosexual" according to my definition of "queer" – as an identity without an essence, not a given condition but a horizon of possibility, an opportunity for self-transformation, a queer potential' (SF 79). In this sense, Halperin's queer is a position open to everyone, not just gay men – because anyone could undergo queering by assuming a marginal social position in order to transform oneself. As an ethical practice, it is personal as much as it is collective, for ethics always involves relations with others, and therefore establishes and multiplies collective styles of life.[8] The politics of queer resistance is about the creative invention of new collective styles of life through ethical practices of self-transformation that are exercised collectively, that is, together with others. Unlike the politics of gay liberation, queer resistance is not about reforming laws or liberating an oppressed or suppressed 'true' gay identity; rather, it is the realisation of the freedom to create a distinctive way of existing.

But what could function as a modern ethical practice of queer resistance, one that realises the subject's freedom by enabling them to relocate from the position of the object to that of the subject, or – what amounts to the same thing – to make subjection into subjectivation? Halperin takes his cue from Foucault's differentiation between desire and pleasure, wherein the former marks a permanent feature of the subject while the latter constitutes an event that transcends subjectivity. As an experience that takes place at the limit of subjectivity, 'pleasure is desubjectivating, impersonal: it shatters identity, subjectivity, and dissolves the subject, however fleetingly, into the sensorial continuum of the body, into the unconscious dreaming of the mind' (SF 95).[9] For Halperin, sexual practices such as sadomasochism, fistfucking and anonymous sexual encounters which Foucault described can therefore be considered as queer practices of self-transformation, because in such practices the subject encounters the otherness of their body, which experiences pleasure in unexpected ways, and discovers multiple erogenous zones beyond the genitalia.[10] In this sense, such practices are forms of desexualisation: the displacement of sexual pleasure and its detachment from the specificity of the genitalia. By experiencing the otherness of one's own body, one forms an ethical relation to oneself. Foucault suggests that these practices can be effective tools to resist modern technologies of power that use sexuality to assign subjects a 'true' unified self and an identifiable form of desire (that is, sexuality, a sexual identity defined by the object of its desire), and that regulate and control our lives by using these very sexual identities against us – since one of the elements that define power-relations, says Foucault, is that '"the other" (the one over whom power is exercised) be thoroughly recognized and maintained to the very end as a person who acts' (SAP 220). The ethics of queer resistance involves one's becoming-other, which was designed to enable one to evade objectification by power's *dispositifs*, especially sexuality – the one that makes us constantly visible to power's objectifying eye, which thereby becomes more able to discipline our bodies to better serve power's interests:

> through the invention of novel, intense, and scattered bodily pleasure, queer culture brings about a tactical reversal of the mechanisms of sexuality, making strategic use of power differentials, physical sensations, and sexual identity-categories in order to create a queer praxis that ultimately dispenses with 'sexuality' and destabilizes the very constitution of identity itself. (SF 96–7)

We can say that by defining queer politics as 'a kind of spiritual exercise, a modern practice of the self' (SF 101) through Foucault's conception of power and of ethical practices of the self,[11] Halperin confirms the inseparability or the codependency of the two senses of his concept of queer: the political and the ethical, the collective and the individual, the critical and the creative, negation and affirmation, being (gay, lesbian, straight) and becoming (other than gay, lesbian, straight). In this sense, even the most private, local act of relating to oneself through bodily pleasure means participating in a collectivity. Such practices enable the creation of new communities and styles of life; new ways of relating to others, of thinking relationships anew, and of imagining the future as different from what is unbearable in the present, so that the possibility of changing the present becomes viable even in the face of plague and death. This is why Halperin makes the claim that the self can function as a strategy of political activism, 'an experiment we perform on ourselves so as to discover our otherness to ourselves in the experience of our own futurity' (SF 106). I would argue that this is also why the use of the first person in *Saint Foucault* is so prevalent: it has nothing to do with the relativism of subjective truths, even as Halperin weaves his own personal anecdotes into his arguments. The 'I' is present as a sign of its persistent disintegration *and* of its resistant re-creation in a becoming-other. It is used as a strategic device against what Foucault called 'the games of truth'[12] of a given formation of power/knowledge that assigns authority and hence value to persons, institutions and bodies of knowledge, thereby misrepresenting things and individuals in terms of empirical, objective facts. The 'I' is an effect of queering, of a political resistance that entails the ethical practice of relating to oneself, or taking care of the self.

However, it is important to note here that the 'I' is not a strategic device in itself, independently of a specific historical formation of power/knowledge; which means that its use not a matter of personal whim but rather of urgency and necessity. The AIDS crisis brought with it new, frightening, discursive and non-discursive strategies of objectification very different from the disciplinary ones Foucault ascribed to the practices of the late eighteenth and early nineteenth centuries. To an extent, these new strategies can be seen as the perfection of old ones. For instance, if nineteenth-century sexual sciences relied heavily on the technique of confession as the 'general standard governing the production of the true discourse on sex' (HV1 63), and therefore as the primary tactic to pathologise and criminalise sexuality, in the age of AIDS, conversely, science no longer needed to rely heavily on seductive techniques that induce one to speak the truth of one's sexuality, because the body does it 'willingly'; the body confesses by betraying visible symptoms, even if the 'I' is silent. This is whence comes the experience of overall self-alienation, of the body's estrangement from itself and from the self often described by survivors of the AIDS crisis: 'the I that is writing now does not understand itself to be the me of that sentence. I am the witness to my body's history. I watch as it becomes ill, from some safe distance, like watching the news on television' (Bordowitz 2004: 145).

Moreover, this unusual partiality for according the body's silent confession the status of truth is especially evident in the early years of AIDS, when physicians concluded that symptoms of AIDS attested to a patient's homosexuality, even in the face of lack of evidence, and even if the patient denied it or remained silent about it, and despite the fact that the number of women diagnosed with the 'gay disease' was increasing.[13] Whatever the 'I' spoke on behalf of itself or a group had no real effect on determining its own being and truth; these were predetermined *for* the I 'objectively'. This is why the I as a strategic device cannot be used to win the game of truth, because at the very moment the I demands recognition, legitimation and rights, it is already defeated – it confirms 'subjectively' that which is visible 'objectively'; it makes its truth ('I am gay') an empirical fact ('you are diseased'). Conversely, Halperin's queer I does not aim to win the game of truth but to subvert it by becoming-other, and I would argue that the most telling sign of this becoming-other is present right at the beginning, when he cries '*Michel Foucault, c'est moi!*' (SF 8).

Sedgwick seemed to anticipate the queer formula of the I as a strategic device, which, a year later in *Saint Foucault*, Halperin would make – through writing – an ethical practice of political resistance:

Philosophically Queer: Constructing a Concept

> 'Queer' seems to hinge much more radically and explicitly [than gay and lesbian] on a person's undertaking particular, performative acts of experimental self-perception and filiation. A hypothesis worth making explicit: that there are important senses in which 'queer' can signify only *when attached to the first person*. One possible corollary: that what it takes – all it takes – to make the description 'queer' a true one is the impulsion *to* use it in the first person. (Sedgwick 1994: 9)

Sedgwick's argument precisely applies to Halperin's use of the first person – it marks not self-indulgence but an impulsion, necessity, urgency. He is *compelled* to become other than himself;[14] but I would argue that in the process Foucault, too, can no longer be himself and must become other – a Saint – so that writing, in turn, can also undergo transformation to become no longer theory in the narrow sense (namely, the consolidation of a system of applicable ideas and principles), nor biography (which shares with the biomedical discourse of AIDS the 'terror of reason' that inheres in the apparatus of description [SF 176]), but rather hagiography: an inventive celebration, through writing, of a different future incarnated in the life and works of a quasi-fictional Saint Foucault. Through writing, then, Halperin undergoes a becoming-hagiographer.[15] In the very act of writing, in its hagiographical style and in the strategic use of the first person, Halperin practises upon and through his self the very same form of queer resistance he ascribes to the practices of ACT UP and to certain desexualising practices.

Hagiographical writing, AIDS activism, desexualisation – these are all contingent local solutions, born out of necessity and struggles of survival, to the same problem: how to resist objectification from within a given formation of power/knowledge. Each solution replays the problem but with a difference, according to its own means. Writing, however, enables Halperin to do philosophy as hagiography, to create the concept of queer not as a final solution, nor as a better or more complete one, but rather as a different take on the problem whereby these practices function as interrelated singularities that make possible the envisioning of a different future. The concept of queer is incarnated in its actualisations yet not exhausted by them: it is both an ideal immanent position, a pure potentiality, a 'horizon of possibility' (SF 62), *and* a series of actualisations that have already been taking place. The critical (constructivist) move, however, does not end here. It began earlier with the critique of false problems, before proceeding to the formulation of the transcendental problem and its queer solution. The next step is to account for the three activities that comprise constructivism: creating concepts, laying out a plane, and inventing a conceptual persona.

Conceptual Personae: The Exemplary Saint

Halperin's use of the first person is a writing strategy that sets in motion a series of transformations or becomings: of Halperin himself, of Foucault and of writing. These becomings are effects of an urgent necessity to think and act differently in the face of crisis and an impossibility in the present – the AIDS crisis, the homophobic strategies of discourses and their coercive means of objectification. If the problem of resisting authority is articulated and rearticulated in the first person throughout *Saint Foucault*, this should not be read as a personal predicament. Importantly, I would argue that the 'I' articulating the problem here gives us a point of view relative neither to a subject nor an actual person, but rather to an open virtual whole that comprises all the variations of the problem. Though Halperin recounts two personal anecdotes to demonstrate the problem he then presents, the real subject of this problem – the perspective through which the problem is deliberated – is not Halperin himself, nor any other actual (gay) person, but rather a 'resurrected' Foucault; as if it is Foucault who speaks through Halperin, or, as he put it in the cry cited earlier: 'in short, *Michel Foucault, c'est moi*' (SF 8). An invented Foucault, Foucault-as-queer-thinker, personifies the problem of gay men demanding the authority to speak, or their laying claim to a position as legitimate subjects of knowledge. Taking another step forward, I argue that Halperin is capable of creating queer as a concept – a solution to the problem of resisting authority – only by letting Foucault mediate his claim. As Deleuze put it, 'mediators are fundamental. Creation's all about mediators . . . I need my mediators to express myself, and they'd never express themselves without me' (N 125). It is this resurrected Foucault that enables Halperin to create queer as a critical philosophical concept, for he plays a principal role in Halperin's philosophical activity, defined here as constructivism.

What exactly is Foucault's role here, and how should we understand Halperin's cry 'Foucault, it is I'? This seemingly self-celebrating statement functions as an enunciation or 'voice' manifested as one of the three activities of constructivism, namely, the constitution of a relative point of view or perspective on the problem, or what Deleuze and Guattari term 'the conceptual personae':

Philosophically Queer: Constructing a Concept

> Conceptual personae are the philosopher's 'heteronyms', and the philosopher's name is the simple pseudonym of his personae. I am no longer myself but thought's aptitude for finding itself and spreading across a plane that passes through me at several places ... The destiny of the philosopher is to become his conceptual persona or personae, at the same time that these personae themselves become something other than what they are historically, mythologically, or commonly ... The conceptual personae is the becoming or the subject of a philosophy, on a par with the philosopher ... the philosophical shifter is a speech-act in the third person where it is always a conceptual personae who says 'I'. (WP 64)

Put simply, when Halperin says 'I', he is saying 'I think *as* Foucault', but also, in a chain of becomings, 'I write *as* hagiographer' and 'I exercise *as* Saint'. In this sense, he is always already writing in the third person. But why does this chain of becomings necessarily occur? 'Conceptual personae carry out the movements that describe the author's plane of immanence, and they play a part in the very creation of the author's concepts' (WP 63), say Deleuze and Guattari; therefore, conceptual personae are the 'powers of concepts' (WP 65). Halperin's Foucault, on the one hand, is not the author's representative,[16] but rather his mask of a tendency or a vector within a different milieu of thought – an impersonal mode of thinking consistent in its own accord; the proper name associated with a new image of thought, or what Deleuze and Guattari call 'a plane of immanence'. But, on the other hand, as such, he is also the instance demanding the creation of adequate concepts that meet the internal conditions of such an image. This is why both author and personae must become-other: they are not representations or expressions of who they 'really' are, their biographical personalities, but rather the conceptual personification of two codependent aspects of a way of thinking incarnated in one conceptual persona; in other words, both the singular constituents of a particular way of thinking *and* the concepts that such way of thinking made possible. The two aspects of a way of thinking presuppose each other: a concept created by thought is already a realisation of the conditions that enabled it, but these conditions, even in their ideality, can only be reached immanently through the created concept. Therefore, if the concept of queer is predicated on what we can call 'Foucauldian thought', this way of thinking does not precede the concept in any way, but is rather constructed alongside it. Halperin ascribes to Foucault a way of thinking that Foucault himself had not laid out explicitly, namely, a thinking where a relation of mutual supposition is formed between politics and ethics. Therefore, I would read Halperin's statement, 'I am well aware that my treatment of [Foucault's] thought is often crude, reductive ... and signally lacking in the subtlety which Foucault himself never ceased to display' (SF 14), as if he was saying that he *invents* a different Foucault, a conceptual Foucault, who can simultaneously provide the ground for a specific way of thinking and render a new concept thinkable. This 'conceptual Foucault' is both the proper name of a thought defined by a certain relation between politics and ethics *and* the first figure of the concept of queer.

In other words, Foucault as conceptual persona is that which links the conditions of the problem to the solution such conditions make possible. The concept of queer can thus solve the problem of resisting authority because queer consists of two distinguished yet inseparable aspects – one political and the other ethical – the relation between which it presupposes. But this in turn means that queer is grounded on Foucauldian thought in which there is no discrepancy between the middle and later Foucault; a thought in which authority, power and knowledge (and a series of other related concepts, such as truth, subjectivity, desire, pleasure) cannot be articulated or 'make sense' without relating to ethical practices of self-fashioning. It is in this sense that Deleuze and Guattari describe conceptual personae as 'intercessors' (or mediators), for they mediate between problems and solutions, and thus between the two other activities of constructivism, namely, creating concepts and laying out a plane of immanence:

> if the concept is a solution, the conditions of the philosophical problem are found on the plane of immanence presupposed by the concept (to what infinite movement does it refer in the image of thought?), and the unknowns of the problems are found in the conceptual personae that it calls up (what personae, exactly?). (WP 80–1)[17]

Thus far it is clear why Halperin, in order to think *as* Foucault, has to become other, and also why Foucault has to become other than himself; but why does Foucault *have to become* a saint, and Halperin a hagiographer? The answer takes us back to the event. In such turbulent times, Halperin is in need of a guide, a mentor, a master, and 'a compelling model for an entire generation of scholars, critics, and activists' (SF 7). Thus, it seems that for Halperin, Foucault is what I would characterise as an *Exemplary Saint*: he whose 'teachings' (his works) and life set an example worthy of emulation. What was it in Foucault that Halperin found so worthy? 'An instructive example of someone whose acute and constantly revised understanding of his own social location enabled him to devise some effective but unsystematic modes of resistance to the shifting discursive and political conditions which circumscribed his own practice' (SF 162). Thus, such a saint is exemplary in the other sense of the word, too: the one who is regarded as a threat to the social order, which will launch an attack against him and *make an example of him*; a warning to his followers, like Christ on the cross. The two senses are inseparable in the case of Saint Foucault: we see him at his best, worthiest of our admiration and attention, precisely when he is being made into an example – when he is criticised, scorned, rejected. This becomes clear in the second essay that comprises *Saint Foucault*, where Halperin offers an impassioned critique of Foucault's biographers, and problematises the genre of biography as a whole, which he describes as 'an offense to the subject's autonomy, a violation of whatever illusions of hermeneutic control over the meaning of her or his existence a subject may have happened to cherish' (SF 136). When Foucault is made into an example, he is at his best also because it is then that we can capture the dynamics of his resistance, his fluctuations in relation to 'the shifting discursive and political conditions which circumscribed his own practice', which mark the varying trajectories of his creative becoming-other.[18] Foucault resists precisely by becoming-other: 'do not ask me who I am, and do not ask me to remain the same: leave it to our bureaucrats and our police to see that our papers are in order' (AK 19). It is from this Exemplary Saint that Halperin seeks guidance: someone who could serve as a model of resistance-by-becoming-other; an ideal personification of his concept of queer.

But with this figure of the Exemplary Saint, two problems come to mind. First, this still does not explain why Foucault has to become a *saint* who is exemplary, and not any other persona – why not a philosopher, an intellectual, a hero, an artist, an outlaw? In other words, what specifically constitutes the relation between exemplarity and saintliness? Secondly, by making Foucault an exemplary saint, does Halperin not compromise his entire anti-authoritarian project? Does Halperin not risk reproducing the very biographical procedure of appropriation and objectification he is so critical of, and risk ending up divesting his subject of autonomy? And by making him a saint, or a spiritual guide, does he not risk restoring – in and through Foucault – the very form of authoritative power which he challenges but to which he may nevertheless find himself submitting?

To address these difficulties, it might prove useful to compare Halperin's Saint Foucault to another conceptual persona of the same type – Jean-Paul Sartre's Saint Genet. Sartre's persona relates to entirely different concepts and planes, and the differences between the two personae will help clarify why Foucault has to become a specific type of saint. Let us first examine the relation constitutive of exemplarity and saintliness. Generally, the Christian canonised saints are all exemplary in their devotion to God, and their ascetic practices are expressions of their devotion – from various forms of self-renunciation to martyrdom.[19] Foucault and Genet, however, are deviant saints, because they denounce or displace God's absolute authority to grant them rightful existence, but retain the form of the saintly practice along with its inevitable personal risk, namely, ascetics. For both Halperin and Sartre the formal characteristic of ascetics is the action of a self upon self, which allows for self-transformation and re-creation; for both, God is replaced with power; and saintliness – as an effect of ascetics – is both an ethical practice inseparable from the political (in my reading of Halperin) or from a 'social fact' (Sartre) and a means for self-fashioning (Halperin) or subjective determination (Sartre).

However, the nature of the ascetic practice is precisely what makes Foucault, but not Genet, an Exemplary Saint: in his ascetic practices – particularly writing, having sex with men and political activism – Foucault never exhausted the potential of subjectivation; on the contrary, he strained it to infinity with each and every actual subjectivating practice, and he never ceases to become-other at the very moment of actualisation. In this sense, he had never reached subjectivity per se, as an end point, only subjectivation as an incessant process of self-transformation and self-creation. He was therefore truly free in the only sense of freedom his thought allows for – immanent freedom unburdened by a sanctioning God or focal points of power. He acquired saintliness as an ideality – the perfect instance of the self-creating Free Person – inasmuch as he was able to elevate himself above actual circumstances. Yet it is an exemplary ideality in the sense that it is always possible to extract the virtual ideal from its actualisations, none of which could be said to be the final word on the ideal. In other words, the ideal never resembles its actualisations (therefore the Platonic metaphysical hierarchy of ideas and copies cannot be used to evaluate them), yet it can only be made recognisable through its actualisations. The Exemplary Saint is not the ideal subject but rather *the ideality of subjectivation as an infinite process of self-creation*; a conceptual personification of constant self-transformation and self-creation from which we can always learn (or follow the example it sets): the ideality of becoming-other-as-self-creation itself undergoes transformation each time it is actualised, yet it never surrenders its ideal form nor resembles its actualisations, for its only rule – its very ideality – is that of transformation. For this reason, I argue that Foucault had to become an Exemplary Saint for Halperin: the more Foucault changed his concepts, his problematics, his attitudes, the more he was an ideal example of becoming-other as the only rule of subjectivation.

Genet, however, is a different kind of saint, one that it is best not to emulate in any way, for his saintliness involves an ethics that Sartre, despite all his admiration, is unwilling to accept: 'if I stand away from it and . . . if I see it as anonymous ethic that is offered up amongst many others, and without any recommendation, I immediately condemn it. And *in every shape and form*' (Sartre 1963: 245–6). Genet is what Sartre calls a Diabolical Saint, not simply because he practises an ethics of evil in which the saint and the evildoer become indistinguishable, and not simply because Genet takes it upon himself to embody and live this impossible contradiction, but because his saintliness is a sham, a ploy:

> It is all rhetoric. He lowers himself in order to elevate himself, but the elevation and the lowering remain symbolic . . . His whole system of Saintliness . . . is based on the following principle: that betrayal effects a metamorphosis in the soul of the betrayer. If we are to believe Genet, he would destroy in order to destroy himself . . . would descend, one by one, the rungs of the ladder of Evil. But the fact is that I don't believe him: he argues with himself, destroys himself symbolically, suffers in the abstract, forgets his suffering, is reborn from his ashes and goes off to love elsewhere. All this intense destructive activity takes place on the spot and without him moving a muscle. (1963: 246–7)

Genet's ethics involves no real action, and therefore his saintliness – despite its being constituted as a practice intended to extract being out of nothingness – will never count as free, nor will it free him from suffering, nor will it make suffering meaningful. Even though Sartre distinguishes Genet from other types of saints (St Theresa as the Canonised Saint and Marcel Jouhandeau as the Sinner Saint), he is eventually equally suspicious of them all, 'always for the same reason, to wit, that it is, to my way of thinking, only the mystical bough of the generosity of consumption' (1963: 246). According to Sartre, saintliness is a phenomenon that was born in consumer societies, where work is no longer a creative activity, but merely the groundwork for ritualistic destruction: the moment of consuming a commodity that both eternalises the destroyed object and 'incorporates it symbolically into its owner in the form of a *quality*' (1963: 196). In these societies, while some play the role of consumers, others will have to find another way to achieve social approval: they will have to become heroes, soldiers or saints – those who choose their own consumption (on the battlefield or by God) in order to realise, in their own self-destruction, the social ideal of consumption. The saint, the 'fine flower of consuming societies' (1963: 200), is a product of the Church's continuing efforts throughout history to reinvigorate the dying aristocratic ethic of 'generosity in consumption' (1963: 198): the wasteful production of goods whose very purpose is for them to be destroyed. 'His [the saint's] extreme destitution and lingering death are not even conceivable without the luxury and myths of a consuming society' (1963: 200), because even in industrial producing societies the ideal of consumption has not disappeared, it was only readjusted and fine-tuned. For the outdated saint to exist, wealth must exist too for him or her to refuse using it, and at the same time announce that he or she is the richest person alive:

> in pursuing Saintliness, it is therefore *something* which they are refusing. But by means of the transport they display in refusing, by means of the self-torture which they practice, they convince themselves and others that they have refused *everything*. And as public destruction involves a public and conspicuous assertion of titles to property, these poor wretches are the richest of men. (1963: 201)

Genet will turn into nothing but the diabolical image of the society that rejected him, a destructive society that finds being only in destruction. But, as a Diabolical Saint, he is entirely defeated – he consummates consumption by fulfilling the very social ideal from which he struggles to free himself. His saintliness will change nothing, not in himself nor in the world: 'abolishing *everything*, it touches *nothing*. Without efficacy, it is, at bottom, merely a kind of rhetoric. The course of the world will not be changed by a few faked states of the soul, a few operations performed on language' (1963: 202). In comparison, my reading of Foucault as Halperin's Exemplary Saint suggests that Foucault succeeds in being exemplary precisely where Genet fails: his ethics affirms his freedom, he resists where power oppresses; he subverts power in his constant movement of becoming-other. For Sartre, Genet resists only to eventually find himself standing still, moving nowhere, changing nothing; and with all the evil he could bring himself to muster, he offends no one. According to Sartre, he would have to undergo two more metamorphoses before he could reclaim freedom.

As saints, both Foucault and Genet are 'out of their time'. For Sartre, Genet is a *passéiste* – his saintliness is outdated, a remnant of a suspicious ethics that therefore cannot be, in principle, exemplary. But for Halperin, I would argue, Foucault can be regarded as a *futuriste* – his saintliness transcends power-relations by affirming itself from within them without recourse to a transcendent order (God, power) or a social ideal. Foucault, like the concept of queer, occupies the point of view of the future – what Halperin describes as a 'horizon of possibility', the real potentiality inherent in power-relations, which is renewed in each and every actualisation (concepts, texts, etc.), that is, in each and every becoming.

The second problem I indicated seems at first glance more difficult to undo, but it is in fact not so complicated. The key is in the third term in the chain of becomings presented earlier – the becoming of writing. It is through writing, so my argument goes, that Halperin enters a becoming-hagiographer, Foucault a becoming-saint, and writing itself a becoming-hagiography. Hagiography does not escape power, nor does it liberate the hagiographer of power; again, a comparison to Sartre's *Saint Genet* is telling – for Halperin, Sartre's book demonstrates how dangerously oppressive writing about the life of another person can be (and this is his only reference to Sartre). Although Sartre's book is not strictly a biography, we could see it as the form of failed hagiography that Halperin is at pains to avoid writing, as he states: 'it is revealing that anyone who understood Genet as Sartre did should nevertheless have gone on to write and publish such a book about him' (SF 135).

In contrast to Sartre's, Halperin's hagiography refuses philosophers' and biographers' transcendent systems of judgement. In celebrating Foucault's saintliness, that is, by fictionalising Saint Foucault, Halperin inevitably surrenders to a style of writing that no longer adheres to the dictums of theoretical argumentation or biographical description, but rather subverts them both. Importantly though, this fictionalisation is inseparable from a political critique of Foucault's biographers in relation not only to the genre of biography, but also to the abusive use of writing that recounts the lives of disempowered people, particularly of gay life: 'the struggle for interpretive authority and for control of representation, intrinsic as it may be to the biographical situation in general, acquires an absolutely irreducible political specificity when it is waged over a gay life' (SF 136). Halperin's way of resisting and extending the anti-authoritarian struggle through writing is to employ several tactics, all of which are subsumed within his becoming-hagiographer: he refuses to participate in biography's games of truth, because he intentionally does not seek to establish the truth of his subject,[20] but rather – like a true hagiographer – to edify his readers and make a believer out of them. In his influential *Legends of the Saints*, hagiographic scholar Hippolyte Delehaye confirms that hagiographies of the Middle Ages, although they often bear on actual historical people and events, are amalgams of facts and myths. Moreover, medieval hagiographers inherited Antiquity's conception of history, where no real difference was made between history and rhetoric, and where 'the historian held as it were a place midway between the rhetor and the poet ... Their historians were concerned above all with literary effectiveness; they gave less consideration to factual truth, and hardly any to exactness' (Delehaye 1962: 52). This explains why writing, if it is to escape and reverse the disciplinary mechanisms of biographical description, cannot involve the establishing of 'the real' or 'alternative' truth, because what makes Saint Foucault exemplary has nothing to do with facts and truth; rather, it has everything to do with a political critique of the strategies of homophobic discourses, and with the possibilities of resistance such mechanisms make available: the creation of a new concept to rethink the possibilities for changing the present, as they are expressed in ACT UP's new form of queer politics of resistance, and in ethical practices that create new styles of life and thus new communities.

In my view, this is where the strategic use of the 'I' can also be seen as reversing the biographers' critical distance from their subject, from which they derive much of their supposedly disinterested authoritative power. Halperin is well aware of this when he criticises Foucault's biographer, James Miller:

> But I do think it is no accident that James Miller, in the interests of preserving his own panoptic privileges, suppressed and evaded the personal and political significance that Foucault's homosexuality and sadomasochism obviously held for him. His *self-effacing* style powerfully confirms the Foucauldian axiom that the methods of disciplinary power, in order to operate successfully, require (and therefore impose) discretion; they cannot survive their own theatricalization. (SF 183, my emphasis)

Philosophically Queer: Constructing a Concept

Against such a self-effacing style, Halperin opts for what I would describe as a hagiographical *self-intensifying* style, where history and legend, critique and creation, author and subject, and the I and the Other cannot be told apart by the standard of truth – on the contrary, it is the very standard of truth that such a style puts into crisis. The hagiographical style undermines the claim to truth not only at the very moment Foucault is made into an example, but when Halperin, too, is made into an example by the personal anecdotes that he weaves into Foucault's part-historical, part-fabricated situation, perceiving himself as risking his own credibility, too. In this sense, then, Halperin cannot be said to repeat the biographical procedure that assumes power over the subject of writing.

He also avoids the risk of restoring authority in and through Foucault. While his political critique of Foucault's biographers exposes their disciplinary strategies of assuming authority over their subject, Halperin's becoming-hagiographer *replays* the problem of authoritative description through its particular solution – hagiography. In other words, Halperin is not unaware of the risk of restoring authority 'in' Foucault (and possibly in himself, as the author of *Saint Foucault*), just as he is aware of the futility of his critique of biography.[21] But he nevertheless creates a possible, particular solution that is wholly derived from and conditioned by the problem of authority and the difficulties it entails. I would argue, then, that Halperin does not restore authority or replace one form of authority (biography) with another (hagiography), but rather *problematises* authority:

> It is problematization that responds to these difficulties, but by doing something quite other than expressing them or manifesting them: in connection with them, it develops the conditions in which possible responses can be given; it defines the elements that will constitute what the different solutions attempt to respond to. This development of a given into a question, this transformation of a group of obstacles and difficulties into problems to which the diverse solutions will attempt to produce a response, this is what constitutes the point of problematization and the specific work of thought. (Foucault, E 118)

Perhaps unwittingly, Halperin's problematisation of authority is very much akin to Foucault's problematisation of his own authority in his 1983 and 1984 series of lectures on *parrēsia* ('free-spokenness'), in which he examines the role of the other in practices of the self, particularly the role of the ancient master.[22] Halperin's critique of biography is inseparable from a creative hagiography, and, combined, both critique and hagiography render concrete another aspect of the problem of authority, which was itself replayed in the first essay by the creation of the concept of queer. By problematising authority rather than claiming it, Halperin is able to formulate the conditions of the problem without ever guaranteeing that any one solution, his or others', can solve it once and for all. He does not shy away from the difficulties that arise with a concept such as queer (SF 64–6), nor with the notion of homosexual sex as a spiritual exercise (SF 107–12), nor with the possibility that what he considers 'queer practices of freedom' can be seen as new forms of disciplinary power (SF 112); there are no prescriptions and no guarantees. But precisely because there are no final solutions, Halperin succeeds in dramatising and intensifying the urgency of the problem, which may push us further to think and rethink other solutions over and over. He openly sides with Foucault, who said that 'my point is not that everything is bad, but that everything is dangerous . . . If everything is dangerous, then we always have something to do' (E 256). This way, Halperin preserves the open-ended, futurist aspect of both Foucault's vision of progressive politics and the concept of queer as that which makes possible the continuous transformation of the present.

The Double-Faced Concept

Deleuze and Guattari explain that 'the features of conceptual personae have relationships with the epoch or historical milieu in which they appear that only psychosocial types enable us to assess' (WP 70). Like the Friend, the Rival, the Idiot, the Madman and other types in Deleuze and Guattari's examples, the Saint can be considered such a psychosocial type endowed with features that vary historically and geographically, but that, importantly, are determined by the plane or the concept:

> The physical and mental movements of psychosocial types, their pathological symptoms, their relational attitudes, and their legal status, become susceptible to a determination purely of thinking and of thought that wrests them from both the historical state of affairs of a society and the lived experience of individuals, in order to turn them into the features of conceptual personae, or *thought-events* on the plane laid out by thought or under the concepts it creates. (WP 70)

In our case, we need to determine how the features of the Exemplary Saint characterise or bear upon a way of thinking that is manifest in the two other activities of constructivism: creating a concept and laying out a plane. By comparing Saint Foucault to Saint Genet, I demonstrated how two completely different ways of thinking result in two different types of saints; in Deleuze and Guattari's terminology, we could even describe one type as 'sympathetic' and the other as 'antipathetic' (we should recall that Sartre denounces Genet's saintliness; in Sartre's case, Genet will be made to transform into two other, more sympathetic, conceptual personae: first, the Aesthete, and finally the Writer). Nevertheless, they both belong to their respective plane and concepts: 'conceptual personae carry out the movements that describe the author's plane of immanence, and they play a part in the very creation of the author's concepts' (WP 63). How can we characterise this saint so far? We know that the Exemplary Saint achieves saintliness not by knowledge (or truth) but by a continual ascetic practice that begins with 'self-renunciation'. Unlike the Diabolical Saint, he does not deprive himself of goods and love; rather, he renounces his own self, he refuses to be the same, so that he can escape that which makes life unbearable in the present by discovering his own otherness within himself. Therefore, the Exemplary Saint discovers new ways to think and live which previously seemed impossible or unthinkable: 'maybe the target nowadays is not to discover what we are but to refuse what we are' (Foucault, SAP 216).

By refusing his self he also refuses authority, and frees himself from authoritative descriptions by making ascetic practice a way of life. In this sense, the Exemplary Saint can also be conceived as another type (or mask) or persona, namely, the Free Person – the one who exercises their freedom by transforming and recreating his- or herself. The Saint/Free Person's ascetic practice expresses both resistance to authority (a denial of the identity imposed upon them) and affirmation of freedom (the free creation and multiplication of new identities). His freedom, or his practices of freedom (ascetics), is what makes Saint Foucault exemplary – a model, a master to learn from, in a double sense: on the one hand, he is exemplary because he is free inasmuch as he resists (not because he achieves total freedom), and his continuous resistance determines his fluctuating degrees of freedom. On the other hand, he is exemplary precisely because he is *not* an ideal Master, yet another figure that substitutes one form of authority for another; rather, he becomes the figure of the problematisation of authority – the master who refuses to determine the truth once and for all; the 'role model' who puts into crisis the very idea of the role model.

In my constructivist account, these general features need to be taken up again – this time from the point of view of thought – so that we can determine the nature of the mode of thinking personified in such an Exemplary Saint, and in what sense this saint can be said to participate in the creation of the concepts that are related to this mode of thinking. As Deleuze and Guattari insist, 'conceptual personae are thinkers, solely thinkers', and so is the Exemplary Saint whose 'personalized features are closely linked to the diagrammatic features of thought and the intensive features of concepts' (WP 69). This statement makes sense only if we construct the respective concept and plane between which the conceptual persona mediates.

Let us now turn to the concept. In what sense are the features of the concept said to be intensive? Concepts are mobile, finite multiplicities: they are comprised of a finite number of components that could themselves be concepts in their own right, and therefore they are open to variation since they can be taken up by other concepts and other problems. What defines a concept is not a general idea nor an empirical object to which it refers, but rather its consistency: the way its components become inseparable though distinct (internal consistency), along with the relations the concept forms with other concepts (external consistency). It is the concept's internal consistency that accounts for its intensive features:

> Each concept will therefore be considered as the point of coincidence, condensation, or accumulation of its own components ... In this sense, each component is an *intensive feature* ... which must be understood not as general or particular but as a pure and simple singularity ... the concept's components are neither constants nor variables but pure and simple *variations* ordered according to their neighborhood ... [The concept] is ordinal, an intension present in all the features that make it up. (WP 20)

The components are intensive in the sense that they are variations, or differences in degree of a single power. For example, let us go back to Deleuze and Guattari's discussion of Descartes's famous concept, the *cogito*. Its three components are *to* doubt, *to* think, *to* be. Expressing the components in the infinitive is simply a way of understanding what Deleuze and Guattari mean when they say that the components are intensive: they are neither general (all the possible ways to think, to doubt, to be) *nor* particular (thinking as imagining, thinking as sensing; being infinitely, being finitely). No matter the case, general or particular, each component is singular (thinking in all its variations cannot be reduced to being in all its variations; and being cannot be reduced to doubting. They are still distinct.) The *cogito*, as a concept of the self, is what orders these three components together (as their point of coincidence and condensation); it keeps them distinct (the heterogeneity of the concept) but also inseparable (overlapping in their connecting points) – there are zones of neighbourhood or thresholds of indiscernibility between the components, where 'something passes from one to the other, something that is undecidable between them' (WP 19–20). The *cogito*, as a concept of the 'I', is that which constitutes the inseparability of its components by establishing zones of indiscernibility between them: 'the first zone is between doubting and thinking (myself who doubt, I cannot doubt that I think), and the second is between thinking and being (in order to think it is necessary to be)' (WP 25).

What are, then, the intensive features of the concept of queer? What are its components and how are they rendered inseparable? Following the formulation of the problem and the solution in Halperin, I redefine 'queer' as *that which resists from a relative position by becoming other than itself, which is to say, by forming a relation to its self*. We have, then, the following components: mobile position, indeterminate selfhood and subsisting otherness. The instability and dynamics of power-relations make every position one assumes within it inherently relative and mobile: any position is a singular point in the network of power-relations, the historical specificity of which determines whether a position is one of the dominated or the dominator. The positions are not fixed even if they seem so, and throughout life one traverses both dominated and dominating positions – we either dominate others or are being dominated by others in different ways and in varying degrees of affectivity (more or less affected by others, more or less affecting others). For instance, we may experience the force of our command as bosses, teachers, leaders; but at the same time we may also experience our weakness as children to our parents, as parents to our children, or as lovers of our partners, in all those situations where the other (the parent, the child, the lover) seem to hold us in their irresistible sway – like the dead parent whose scorn or expectations keep haunting one from the grave; the child whose cry strikes fear in one's heart or makes one feel helpless; the gaze or the smile or the timbre of one's lover's voice that overwhelms one with joy or sorrow. In this sense, the mobile position is a singularity – *a* or *some* position that is neither particular nor general, for 'in the concept there are only ordinate relationships . . . and the concept's components are neither constants nor variables but pure and simple *variations* ordered according to their neighborhood' (WP 20). In other words, as a component or an intensive feature of the concept, the mobile position subsumes *all* the possible positions one can be made to inhabit, all the 'sites' where one affects or is being affected by others, dominates or is being dominated by others, to varying degrees. If we were to articulate it in the infinitive, we would describe the mobile position as 'to be positioned'.[23] It is important to note that one never begins by positioning oneself but only by being positioned; and even if one eventually manages to position oneself, one might not be able to predict or prevent the transformations of power-relations that might transpose one into a different position.[24]

Each position implicates a self that is constituted by power-relations, or more to the point, by what Foucault called 'techniques of domination'; but there are other kinds of techniques, too, that make us relate differently to ourselves, resulting in different forms of subjectivity. Subjectivity, then, is not a personal identity or a substance, but the multiplicity of forms by which one constitutes oneself as a subject: 'undoubtedly, there are relationships and interferences between these different forms of the subject; but we are not dealing with the same type of subject. In each case, one plays, one establishes a different type of relationship to oneself' (E 290). Halperin adopts Foucault's conception of the self and argues that the self 'is not a personal identity so much as it is a relation of reflexivity, a relation of the human subject to itself in its power and its freedom' (SF 75–6). Selfhood partially overlaps a relative, mobile position assigned to it by power-relations, as techniques of domination establish a zone of indiscernibility between the mobile position and the selfhood made possible by power. Selfhood is indeterminate because it is multiplied to infinity by the number of positions it is made (and could be made) to inhabit in a given formation of power: I am gay, I am white, I am a woman, I am a leftist, I am a scholar and so forth. But the self is determined not only by techniques of domination but also by techniques of the self, or the diverse ways in which the self acts upon itself. Selfhood, then, receives a double genesis, or is a product of two distinctive though interpenetrating techniques: on the one hand, it is constructed passively by techniques of domination; on the other hand, it constructs itself actively by techniques of the self. We have already seen that the mobile position also has two codependent aspects: it is a site of both dominating and being dominated, where exercising power necessarily implies points of resistance.[25] In the

Philosophically Queer: Constructing a Concept

concept of queer, then, a second zone of indiscernibility is established between the mobile position and selfhood: that is, between points of resistance and techniques of the self. It is the concept of queer that effects a partial overlap between the respective double aspects of the mobile position and selfhood. Queer makes these two components inseparable so that we cannot understand selfhood independently of its construction by the relative position imposed on it; but we also cannot understand the relative position independently of the process of the self acting upon itself, which at any given moment is capable of transforming a point of power into a point of resistance, or a state of being dominated into a state of domination in one and the same position.

This zone of indiscernibility between the two components (in their double aspects) expresses what I described earlier as the relation of mutual supposition between politics and ethics, or between resistance and subjectivation, in the concept of queer, wherein 'points of resistance' are the site where the self acts upon itself (or where the self practises an ascetics of self-transformation), and wherein 'points of power' (in the sense of domination) are the site where the self is acted upon or is constructed as an effect of techniques of domination. However, the relation between politics and ethics described here is contingent on *this* specific construction of the concept of queer, and it does not have the power of necessity outside this construction. Nothing in principle can guarantee that techniques of the self will not transform into techniques of domination. For example, I may practise veganism as a means to transform myself into a better and healthier person, but this very practice could easily become a means to control and even terrorise non-vegans. The relation *becomes* necessary in the way the concept of queer 'orders' politics and ethics in zones of proximity, so that the only way queer can be said to resist is by saying that it already inhabits a mobile position that is in the process of being transformed from a position of disempowerment to a point of resistance, and that it therefore involves the transformation of selfhood by turning subjection into subjectivation. Queer is the point of coincidence of these two transformations or movements, the zone of their overlapping. I would also argue that queer thus adds a specific sense to what Foucault called 'government'. If government names 'the contact point' where techniques of domination interact with techniques of the self – or 'a versatile equilibrium, with complementarity and conflicts between techniques which impose coercion and processes through which the self is constructed or modified by himself' (Foucault, POT 154) – then queer names a particular form of government or such contact point, where being governed by others is reversed by or transforms into governing oneself; and where this sort of transformation can only be named resistance from the point of view of politics, and subjectivation from the point of view of ethics.

This adds another sense to the indeterminacy of selfhood and to the relativity of the position, namely, the sense of a process or a change taking place. In the concept of queer, both components relate to movement – they are processes of transformation, which is why queer simultaneously captures the double aspect of each component. Queer can be said to be 'an identity without essence' or a pure 'positionality', in Halperin's words, only if we take into consideration the transformation of the mobile position (the point of view of politics) that is *in the process of* being emptied from its positive content.[26] At the same time, queer can also be said to be a spiritual exercise, a practice of self-fashioning, only if we take into consideration the transformation of selfhood (the point of view of ethics) that recreates itself in new contents by acting upon itself. Ultimately the concept of queer 'speaks' both these transformations at the same time, which in my view explains why Halperin can eventually say, without risking contradiction, that 'queer politics itself, finally, is a kind of spiritual exercise, a modern practice of the self' (SF 101). There is no contradiction here between politics and ethics, or mobile position and selfhood, or 'identity without essence' and 'practice of the self'; but there is also no Hegelian sublation of the two, only 'zones of coincidence' where 'something passes from one to the other, something that is undecidable between them' (WP 19–20): selfhood marks the transformation of a mobile position from a point of coercive power into a point of resistance, and the relative position marks the transformation of selfhood from a state of subjection (the self affected by others) to a process of subjectivation (the self affecting itself). That which prevents these two components from being conflated or sublated or falling back on one another, I argue, is the third and final component of the concept – namely, subsisting otherness – which enables the incorporation of the two processes of transformation into a single formula: queer is resistance by becoming-other.

Otherness here, as the third component, is a tricky one. It is not a central concept in Foucault's thought as it is for other philosophers (such as Sartre and Levinas),[27] and it plays a more central role only in Foucault's later writings, particularly in his *Hermeneutics of the*

Philosophically Queer: Constructing a Concept

Subject and *Government of Self and Others*, which were published in France many years after the publication of Halperin's *Saint Foucault*. In these texts, the other simply stands for 'other people' who are not myself, and the problem Foucault addresses is how do relations to oneself involve, implicate and affect one's relations with others. In the construction of the concept of queer, I argue that three distinct senses of otherness should first be distinguished if we are to account fully for the intensive features of the concept, despite these three senses not being distinguished in Halperin's conception. The first sense is a skeletal concept of the non-self, simply 'other people' as they appear in Foucault's later works. I mentioned earlier that power-relations, in Foucault's and Halperin's view, require a recognisable other over whom power is to be exercised, which leads me to the second sense: the other as an object of power. Queer partially retains this sense of otherness, for the second sense refers to the starting point of queer's transformation – the state from which queer departs, the identity it disintegrates, the 'positive content' of the mobile position or the identity that queer empties. But queer does not retain this form of otherness exclusively, otherwise 'becoming other' would only mean that queer affirms itself as a recognisable, self-identical, fixed subject that is nevertheless an object of power, which is what Halperin designates as 'gay'.[28] Rather, there is a third sense of otherness that marks 'a radically impersonal self that can serve as a vehicle for self-transformation because, being nothing in itself, it occupies the place of a new self which has yet to come into being' (SF 104).

These three senses of otherness also explain why I argue that otherness 'subsists': otherness *resides within* selfhood; it is an impersonal self, a dimension that transcends the self yet is nevertheless internal to the self, for it marks the limit of selfhood beyond which it does not remain the same. It therefore defines the transformation of the self, the self's becoming other by multiplying itself from within. Yet otherness also subsists or resides within the mobile position as an object of power – it renders determinable the possibilities for exercising both power and resistance in a given formation of power-relations. But in relation to both the mobile position and selfhood, otherness simply subsists in the sense of *existing independently* as 'other people' – those whose existence power must presuppose if it is to take them as its object (and in this sense, as Foucault argued, otherness is also a condition of power); and those whose existence selfhood must presuppose for it to have a sense of the non-self to begin with (and in this sense, otherness constitutes

A DELEUZIAN CRITIQUE OF QUEER THOUGHT

selfhood's own limits). Only so constructed can we finally argue that otherness has a zone of indiscernibility with each of the two other components: 1) with selfhood, because otherness is both its limit and potential of change, that is, that which both transcends the self and serves as its 'object' (an impersonal self) in the acts of the self acting upon itself; 2) with the mobile position, because otherness functions as both the object upon which power is exercised and as the condition for any exercise of power. Importantly, then, the third component cannot be reduced to either of the two other components, because otherness's third sense – 'other people' – keeps it somewhat independent of both, for it irrefutably subsists or 'just is': the mere existence of other people as both a condition of power and as the limit of the self. Otherness, therefore, is what keeps the two other components from being conflated; what safeguards their relation of mutual supposition. The transformational process that is 'resistance' or 'subjectivation' (depending on the point of view – political or ethical, respectively) necessarily passes through otherness.

The concept of queer is the condensation point of all three components, where they become inseparable by forming zones of indiscernibility with one another, as illustrated in Figure 2.1. Queer is a concept

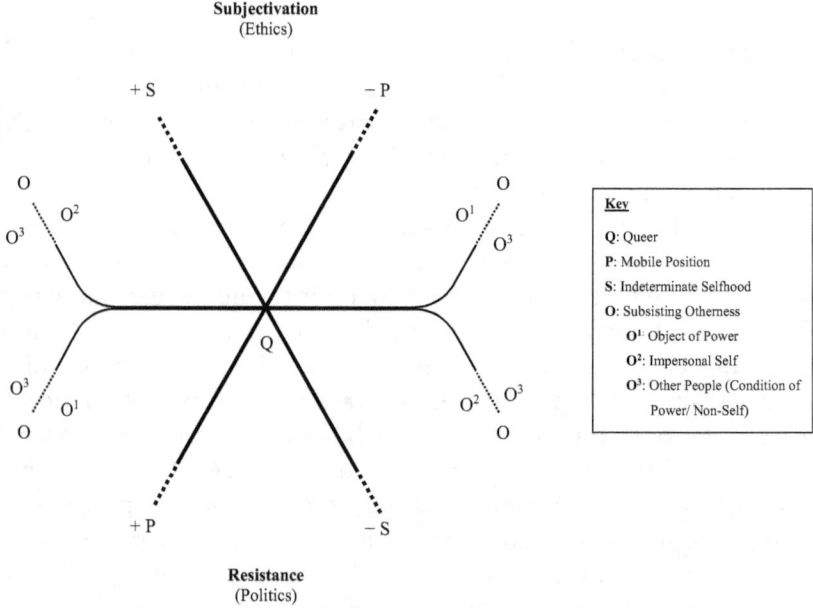

Figure 2.1 Components of the concept.

in which resisting authority takes place through subjectivation, and it defines the process or the movement through which one relocates oneself from the position of the object to that of the subject and therefore realises one's freedom. But as such, queer is not determined by the end point or the starting point of the process; rather, it marks them both as the two poles of a single process – transformation/ transposition. Consequently, the process that takes place between the starting point and the end point is doubled by two points of view: that of resistance and that of subjectivation. In Figure 2.1, the concept of queer (Q) retains two variations of the mobile position (–P, +P), two variations of selfhood (–S, +S), and three variations (O^1, O^2, O^3) of otherness (O). From the point of view of resistance, the mobile position is the site where power is exercised (+P) and at the same time where selfhood disintegrates and becomes an identity without essence (–S). From the point of view of subjectivation, the mobile position is the site of its own transformation into a point of resistance (–P) and at the same time where selfhood recreates itself in a new identity (+S). It is important to note that the plus and minus signs do not mark the same kind of transformation in the mobile position and in selfhood. Selfhood undergoes a *quantitative* change, where –S marks the disintegration of or process of 'emptying' identity, and +S marks the re-creation of a new identity. The mobile position, however, undergoes a *qualitative* change where +P marks a position where power is being exercised over an identity, while –P marks the failure of the exercise of power as that same position becomes a point of resistance. Yet both processes are made possible only by traversing otherness in its three variations: facing the mobile position, otherness appears as the object of power (O^1) yet subsists as 'other people', that is, as the condition of power (O^3). Facing selfhood, otherness appears as an impersonal self or its potential of change (O^2), yet subsists as 'other people,' or as selfhood's rudimentary sense or experience of non-self (O^3).

Thought and Freedom

'Concepts', says Ian Buchanan, 'are not what the philosophers think about, but what they think with' (2000: 48), and yet they are never freestanding because they presuppose a plane of immanence. In other words, the creation of concepts involves at the same time a laying out of 'the very conditions of the thinkability of a concept' (2000: 57). Deleuze and Guattari define the plane of immanence as 'the image of thought, the image thought gives itself of what it means to think, to make use of thought, to find one's bearings in thought' (WP 37). At first glance, it would seem simple to determine Halperin's plane or image of thought – we could say that his is a Foucauldian one, just as earlier I mentioned that with the conceptual persona of Saint Foucault, Halperin says 'I' as if he were saying 'I think as Foucault'. Leaving aside the problem of determining Foucault's thought 'as such' – as if it were one and the same thought in all his writings – which makes such a simple determination impossible, we are still left with the problem of how a Foucauldian way of thinking can be said to create a concept such as queer which does not belong to it; and, moreover, how could such a concept form a new relation between the two different Foucauldian notions of politics and ethics without transforming the Foucauldian image of thought? Put simply, can Halperin be said to be thinking *as* Foucault if at the same time he creates a non- or extra-Foucauldian concept that entails the transformation of the Foucauldian image of thought?

The simple answer is yes:

> philosophers can create new concepts while remaining on the same plane and presupposing the same image as an earlier philosopher whom they invoke as their master . . . However, in every case, this involves extending the original plane by giving it new curves, until a doubt arises: is this not a different plane that is woven in the mesh of the first one? (WP 57)

Halperin's concept of queer and Foucault's concepts, such as power-relations, subjectivation, cultivating a relation to oneself, pleasure and others, belong to the same plane; they are 'concepts of the same group' (WP 58), even though they were created in different times by different authors. This proximity of queer to other Foucauldian concepts constitutes queer's external consistency as a concept. In the previous section I described how zones of indiscernibility between components guarantee the internal consistency of the concept, and yet on the plane, the concept's 'external neighborhood or exoconsistency is secured by the bridges thrown from one concept to another when the components of one of them are saturated' (WP 90). Queer, as a concept, immanently constitutes new relations between Foucauldian concepts in the oscillating movement between resistance and subjectivation, politics and ethics, techniques of domination and techniques of the self. It is this particular movement – the saturation of the concept by the zones of neighbourhood formed between its components – that transforms the Foucauldian image of thought by creating new or different relations between Foucauldian concepts. What I attempt to account for here is precisely this movement of back and forth between queer and other concepts; or, put differently, I attempt to determine the 'diagrammatic features' of the plane, as Deleuze and Guattari put it, for 'thought demands "only" movement that can be carried to infinity. What thought claims by right, what it selects, is infinite movement or the movement of the infinite. It is this that constitutes the image of thought' (WP 37).

To determine what infinite movement thought claims by right in the construction of the concept of queer, it might prove easier to begin with what marks thought's 'negative movement', or what thought rejects, since 'images of thought cannot arise in any order whatever because they involve changes of orientation that can be directly located on the earlier image' (WP 58). The key to understanding Halperin's image of thought is found in the discussion that opens the second chapter of *Saint Foucault*, where he distinguishes between a liberal and a Foucauldian concept of power. In liberal thought, argues Halperin, power is opposed to freedom, for power is identified with the capacity of oppressors to impose their will on other people. But in Foucauldian thought there is no opposition between the two. For Foucault, power is nothing but a relation, or power-relations: 'power is what characterizes the complex relations among parts of a particular society . . . as relations of ongoing struggle. Power is thus a dynamic *situation* . . . a strategic, unstable relation' (SF 17).[29] In this sense, Foucault famously argued, power is everywhere but so is freedom:

> we are always in this kind of situation. It means that we always have possibilities, there are always possibilities of changing the situation. We cannot jump *outside* the situation, and there is no point where you are free from all power relations . . . So what I've said does not mean that we are always trapped, but that we are always free. (E 167)[30]

Against Foucault's liberal critics, who believed that his concept of power 'effectively robbed people of freedom and made successful political opposition impossible' (SF 16),[31] Halperin sides with Foucault and argues that it is precisely the liberal concept of freedom that should be considered as dangerously imposing. The reason is that power in the modern liberal state actually depends on freedom to secure and maintain its hold over its subjects:

the state no longer needs to frighten or coerce its subjects into proper behavior; it can safely leave them to make their own choices in the allegedly sacrosanct private sphere of personal freedom which they now inhabit, because within that sphere they *freely and spontaneously* police both their own conduct and the conduct of others. (SF 18–19)[32]

Foucault's critique of liberal thought enables Halperin in turn to distinguish between two types of struggles in the domain of sexual politics by relating each to a historical movement: the struggle for liberation represented by the Gay Liberation movements, and the struggle for resistance represented by ACT UP. In accord with what Foucault called 'the repressive hypothesis', the struggle for sexual liberation fights to free sexuality *from* power conceived to be embodied in institutional laws, government policies and other discursive and non-discursive practices. What the Gay Lib movements (and other sexual liberation movements of the 1960s and 1970s) sorely miss, according to Foucault, is their own compliance with the modern regime of sexuality, which has *required* and *demanded* since the eighteenth century that we confess again and again, and in numerous contexts, the truth of our sexuality, so that power can tighten its grasp over our lives without our experiencing any form of coercion (HV1 23, 61).[33] Consequently,

> liberation movements bind us more closely to the very thing from which we may need most urgently to emancipate ourselves. What we ultimately have to liberate ourselves from may be nothing less than 'freedom' itself – that is, from the liberal concept of freedom as a regulative or normative ideal of responsible and self-respecting human conduct. (SF 20–1)

Conversely, struggles for resistance realise freedom *within* power, for there is freedom where there is power, and thus there are as many occasions for resistance as there are instances where power is exercised. Such a struggle does not limit itself solely to fighting institutions,[34] but takes place in multiple sites where it devises its own counter-strategies to reverse coercive technologies of domination.[35] 'ACT UP', says Halperin, 'would seem to furnish a perfect example of a strategic power reversal, a form of resistance made possible by the very apparatuses of power/knowledge it was invented to resist' (SF 28–9). He only mentions ACT UP's multiple tactics, and though he does not expand on it later, ACT UP will remain throughout *Saint Foucault* the primary example of queer politics of resistance that Halperin thoroughly opposes to Gay Liberation politics.

Philosophically Queer: Constructing a Concept

However, I would argue that resistance is not what constitutes Halperin's image of thought – resistance, much like power, is a concept, and therefore it should not be confused with the plane of immanence. Deleuze and Guattari are very clear on this point (WP 39–40), for when a concept is confused with its plane, the result is the 'illusion of universals' (WP 49), in which immanence is no longer immanent to itself but rather immanent to something else (like consciousness in the case of Kant), which is itself nothing but a concept. But before I expand on Halperin's plane, I will point out another difficulty that affirms my contention that resistance cannot be identified with the plane. We already know that the concept of queer is double-faced, or that it comprises two points of view: that of politics and that of ethics. Once the construction of queer as a philosophical concept requires taking into account Halperin's detailed discussion of queer aesthetics of existence, we immediately see that resistance is a concept that applies only to the political point of view of the concept of queer, and that it forms the negative pole (the negation of the normative, the process of emptying identity out of the mobile position), which is in direct reciprocal relation to the positive pole of ethics (the sense in which resistance can be said to be productive and not just destructive; the creation of new identities through subjectivation). Resistance, therefore, is no more a plane than subjectivation; both are concepts that inform the components of the concept of queer as a whole. Rather, the movement between resistance and subjectivation, the very movement that is constitutive of queer as a concept, is that which belongs to the plane 'by right'; because for the concept of queer to function as it does – as an incessant movement between resistance and subjectivation that is secured internally by the inseparability of the components – or, in other words, for the statement 'queer is resistance by becoming other' to be meaningful as the complete statement of the concept, something must enable the movement between the two poles of the concepts; something like a condition or a presupposition must already (or simultaneously) be laid out so that such a dynamic relation between the two poles becomes thinkable. If the concept of queer is thinkable as resistance by means of becoming-other, and if, as such, it consists of two points of view that are in a relation of mutual supposition and reciprocation, then the movement between these two aspects is conditioned on the plane; or, what amounts to the same thing, the cause of this movement is to be found on the plane.

Inasmuch as this movement is conditioned on the plane, the plane can be considered to be pre-philosophical:

> it [the plane] is presupposed not in the way that one concept may refer to others but in the way that concepts themselves refer to a nonconceptual understanding . . . Prephilosophical does not mean something preexistent but rather something *that does not exist outside philosophy*, although philosophy presupposes it. These are its internal conditions. (WP 40–1)

For Deleuze and Guattari, this is true of both the absolute plane of immanence, the 'One-All' that includes all the concepts, and of the many planes that have been created throughout the history of philosophy. There is no contradiction nor hierarchy between the one and the many. Philosophy exists in a 'stratigraphic time' (WP 58), where all the planes or images of thought are superimposed on one another, like layers or strata: 'philosophy is becoming, not history; it is the coexistence of planes, not the succession of systems' (WP 59). My goal in this section is not to determine the absolute plane, which is unthinkable in its totality although it must be presupposed, for where there are concepts one also finds some image (of thought) already at work that determines thinkability as such.[36] Rather, my goal is to determine Halperin's image of thought, and what makes queer a thinkable philosophical concept, or, in other words, what guarantees the external consistency of the concept. To this end, we need to determine what enables the specific movement between the two points of view, which is both internal to the concept and nevertheless originates from outside the concept – from its conditions of thinkability.

Formulating the pre-philosphical is one possible point of entry to examining the plane. One of the aspects of the pre-philosphical is an implied presupposition: 'philosophy defined as the creation of concepts implies a distinct but inseparable presupposition' (WP 41). One of Deleuze's examples here and elsewhere is subjective understating, which is presupposed by Descartes's concept of *cogito*.[37] What would be queer's non-conceptual presupposition that makes all of its components inseparable in the movement back and forth between its two points of view, each of which also doubles it?[38] That is, on what condition could resistance and subjectivation be said to be linked in one and the same movement of becoming? When Halperin distinguishes between gay and queer, he says that one can either be or not be gay, but also that 'one can marginalize oneself; one can transform oneself; one can become queer', and

Philosophically Queer: Constructing a Concept

that such willing self-transformation forms the basis of 'queer ethic' (SF 79). Earlier too, he explained the possibility of resistance in terms of a conscious decision to practise resistance by 'assuming and empowering a marginal positionality – not in rehabilitating an already demarcated, if devalued, identity but in taking advantage of the purely oppositional location homosexuality has been made to occupy' (SF 61). There seems to be, then, a subjugated yet persistently *active* person or 'entity', for want of a better term, which is capable of deciding freely, as if by onself, to transform oneself in order to resist being dominated and to create for oneself a new identity. We might be tempted to think that Halperin falls prey to the liberal image of thought he is so eager to escape, wherein personal freedom always precedes power, supposedly because humans are conscious beings that are capable of self-reflection and thus can always change and transcend the circumstances of their lives. However, Halperin, like Foucault, insists that freedom and resistance are not external to power (SF 48), and that ethical practice is a stylisation of freedom 'consisted in freely imposing on the form of one's life a distinctive shape and individual style, and thereby transforming oneself in accordance with one's own conception of beauty and value' (SF 69–70). Such statements, then, take freedom as their presupposition or condition, and such a presupposition, I argue, is entirely commensurable with Foucault's thought without recourse to liberal thought (we shall see why in the discussion that follows). Therefore, my contention is that *freedom is the pre-philosophical ground for Halperin's conceptualisation of queer* – the movement carried to infinity that 'thought claims by right' (WP 37), and is therefore queer's internal condition of thinkability as a concept. Concisely, this means that the concept of queer presupposes that free thought constitutes what it means to think, namely, that thinking depends, for example, not on thought's natural affinity with truth as in the classical image of thought (WP 53), but rather on thought's absolute freedom to move by and for itself, unobstructed. This also means that the opposite statement characterises the plane just as much: circumscription or confinement express what is negative in thought (just as error does when truth expresses thought's positive feature in the classical image of thought).

Consequently, freedom in the concept of queer precedes both power-relations *and* subjectivity; it is not that there is first a free subject whose freedom is then robbed or limited by power, as liberal thought would have it; rather, in Foucault's work, freedom is both the precondition of power and the impetus for the ethical practice of subjectivation. However, this also means that freedom, as the movement that constitutes the plane of immanence, is *not* a concept, and thus we need to determine in what sense it can be said to be the pre-philosophical and even the non-philosophical ground for thought. I will first expand on the immediate sense in which freedom functions as a presupposition both for Foucault and for the philosophical concept of queer, and then I will return to the claim that freedom is not a concept but what constitutes the plane, because, as will be made clear, the presupposition of freedom by the concept of queer will then become a problem that transforms both the concept and the plane.

A conclusion that must be drawn from my construction of queer thus far is that one cannot resist nor can one transform oneself or recreate oneself *unless one is already free* – this is the correlative statement, from the point of view of presupposition, of my redefinition of queer (after Halperin) presented earlier: queer resists from a relative position (within power-relations) by becoming other than itself (in the ethical practice of self-fashioning). Freedom is then a presupposition shared by both points of view that inform the concept – resistance and subjectivation – and, so my argument goes, freedom is that which defines the dynamics of the concept, the movement back and forth between resistance and subjectivation that enables us to say that queer resists and undergoes subjectivation at one and the same time, or in 'infinite speed' as Deleuze and Guattari would put it; as if by saying 'queer' we are saying 'resistance' *and* 'subjectivation' at the same time (but not that they are the same thing, because they are two different aspects irreducible to one another).

Let us consider first in what sense one is already free from each point of view. According to Foucault, if one resists power, one is already free: 'power is exercised only over free subjects, and only insofar as they are free. By this we mean individual or collective subjects who are faced with a field of possibilities in which several ways of behaving, several reactions and diverse comportments may be realized' (SAP 221). Foucault can make such an argument because he distinguishes between power and states of domination: power is defined as 'a mode of action which does not act directly and immediately on others. Instead, it acts upon their actions' (SAP 220), and in this sense power is everywhere – it exists as a 'total structure' wherever people try to affect, block or modify the actions of other people. But this also means that those whose actions are being acted upon are also capable of acting back, so as to impede or overthrow the power exercised over their actions or their possibilities for action.

States of domination, however, are situations whereby it is no longer possible to act back, because

> power relations, instead of being mobile, allowing the various participants to adopt certain strategies modifying them, remain blocked, frozen. When an individual or social group succeeds in blocking a field of power relations, immobilizing them and preventing any reversibility of movement by economic, political, or military means, one is faced with what may be called a state of domination. (E 283)

Enslavement or totalitarian regimes are states of domination.

Queer, as a concept of resistance, occurs in situations of power-relations rather than states of domination, that is, queer applies to or concerns only situations in which one experiences someone or something acting upon one's actions in an attempt to modify or limit them, but at the same time one is not completely disempowered and is able to react. Foucault associated power-relations with the situation of 'agonism'[39] that is dependent, as some commentators observe, on 'concrete spaces of freedom' where exists a tension between the exercise of power and resistance: 'such a point might be thought of as a *stasis* point between the relations of power and the forces of resistance and be characterized as a point of possibility' (Phillips 2002: 336). For Halperin, the immediate sense of queer resistance is the movement, within power-relations, from the position of the object to that of the subject. The nature of this movement or transformation can only be called 'resistance' because it necessarily traverses a concrete space of freedom wherein the possibility of moving from one position to another exists in the first place. Being in the position of the object does not mean that one *is* an object – an object does not resist, it is completely dominated as an obedient automaton (Phillips 2002: 335); rather, being in the position of the object means that one is experiencing an exercise of power in the form of objectification, which is nothing but a technique of domination, an action upon one's actions. So from the point of view of resistance, or in relation to the movement that occurs within the mobile position, we see that resistance is immanent to power-relations, but power-relations do not exist independently of points of resistance that are the site of counteractions against the actions designed to neutralise them. But both the exercise of power and resistance presuppose freedom as a point of uncertainty that makes both possible. Queer, then, is a concept that belongs to this situation of agonism, and therefore must take freedom as its condition.

If power-relations are conditioned by concrete spaces of freedom, or real possibilities to reverse any given agonistic situation, then so are the agents that take part in this situation. In this sense, as Foucault said, power is only exercised over free subjects. This does not mean that he finds people essentially and universally free independently of power. From the point of view of resistance, they are free as agents taking part in an agonistic situation conditioned by freedom. However, they are free in another sense as well. Paul Patton argues that Foucault presupposes the capability of human beings to transform themselves, and that, therefore, the Foucauldian subject should be understood strictly as a subject of action, 'a being capable of acting, capable of responding in one way rather than another to a given situation' (Patton 1989: 268). The subject's capacity to act and react is not homogeneous and universal, but rather it has received different determinations throughout history. Foucault himself frequently denied any a priori (humanist) conceptions of the subject. As Patton puts it, freedom is nothing but the subject's 'power to' (1989: 270) – the agent's power to act in a certain way: 'for Foucault, it is only the thin conception of agency which is involved in the idea of a being free to act, in the minimal, positive sense of the term "free". In this sense, Foucault says, power presupposes freedom' (1989: 271).

With the notion of the free subject, we have moved to the point of view of ethics or subjectivation, where we encounter a crucial obstacle for determining the queer concept's image of thought: instead of having both resistance and subjectivation conditioned by freedom, or instead of freedom's being constitutive of the movement back and forth between the two points of view, it might seem that freedom is the condition of concrete ethical practice, and hence, in principle, that ethics precedes both resistance and the agonistic situation. In other words, freedom seems to constitute a unilateral movement from ethics to politics or from subjectivation to resistance, because the freedom that conditions resistance is a derivative of subjectivation, which is not so much conditioned on freedom as it takes freedom as its quality – as if subjectivation is essentially a free process. This is problematic because it would mean that instead of freedom's being a movement that links the two poles of the concept dynamically and infinitely (so that queer could be said to mean both resistance and subjectivation at one and the same time), freedom rather becomes immanent *to* subjectivation which thereby achieves a transcendent status. We find ourselves back in the Kantian idea of an a priori human consciousness, and with the humanist, existential or liberal notion of an essentially universal free subject (or true inner self) that exists beyond and above any historical formation of power-relations, and that is constituted by the subject's supposedly autonomous capacity to self-reflect and thus self-transform. I will now turn to elaborate this argument step by step.

Let us recall that the concept of queer becomes internally consistent through the inseparability of its components, which together conjoin two distinctive points of view. Earlier I argued that this relation between the two points of view has no necessity in itself – it is a constructed link that for Halperin regains necessity and urgency in the age of AIDS, for AIDS brought into crisis the political efficacy of sexual politics and its strategies. As I indicated earlier, Foucault himself admitted late in his life that the relation between political resistance and ethical practice was still underdeveloped in his work, yet he did believe that thinking such a link is called for in our present:

> When today we see the meaning, or rather the almost total absence of meaning, given to some nonetheless very familiar expressions which continue to permeate our discourse – like getting back to oneself, freeing oneself, being oneself, being authentic etcetera – when we see the absence of meaning and thought in all of these expressions we employ today, then I do not think we have anything to be proud of in our current efforts to reconstitute an ethic of the self ... and in the movement we now make to refer ourselves constantly to this ethic of the self without ever giving it any content, I think we may have to suspect that we find it impossible today to constitute an ethic of the self, even though it may be an urgent, fundamental, and politically indispensable task, if it is true after all that there is no first or final point of resistance to political power other than in the relationship one has to oneself. (HS 251–2)

I think that Foucault's words could also describe the challenge or the impossibility to which Halperin's concept of queer responds: the reforming of the relation between political resistance and ethical self-fashioning. By taking up this challenge, Halperin can truly be considered a philosopher, or a creator of concepts. As Deleuze put it, 'a creator's someone who creates their own impossibilities, and thereby creates possibilities' (N 133). The concept of queer can be said to vivify this relation, because such a relation did exist in the past, in Ancient Greece and Rome, in a specific form and under specific historical circumstances. For example, Foucault indicates that in Plato's *Alcibiades* the theme of 'taking care of oneself' (as a form of the relationship one has with oneself) is perceived as a condition for political action and the exercise of power over other people – one must take care of oneself if one wants to be a ruler of the *polis* (HS 36).[40] But this theme of taking care of oneself, of transforming oneself into a work of art in order to be able to act politically, is no longer available to us today in the same manner – it has changed throughout history,[41] and today we are left with a meaningless, empty form of ethic of the self. However, neither Foucault nor Halperin are suggesting the restoration of the ancient practices of the care of the self; rather, they rediscover these ancient practices as that which constitutes the difference of their present, and therefore as a possible trajectory for rethinking the present and inventing new ways to organise relationships between people and to act politically. So queer revives the ancient relation between political resistance and ethical practice not in the sense of reproducing it,[42] but in the sense of 'bringing it to life' in a new form: one in which political resistance is realised through subjectivation (or the becoming-other of the self that recreates itself), but also in which the ethical practice of subjectivation functions as political resistance, as it takes place in an agonistic situation determined by given power-relations. Social change thus becomes an effect of an autonomous and free process of self-transformation, but self-transformation is politically meaningless outside given power-relations that distribute 'concrete spaces of freedom' or points of uncertainty and possibility in which self-transformation could take place.

The question is whether or not Foucauldian thought can serve as the ground for such a relation, and hence for the concept of queer at all; that is, whether or not Halperin succeeded in transforming Foucauldian thought without falling back on the humanist presuppositions of liberal thought about human nature that both he and Foucault are critical of. The test would be whether he managed to overcome what some critics consider an incommensurable break between the middle and late Foucault,[43] or between two seemingly contradictory concepts of power that are present in his work, and their ramifications for his conception of the subject. Paul Patton convincingly argued that such criticisms confuse Foucault's concept of power with domination, thereby failing to understand how power can be said, on the one hand, to create subjects and delimit the range of possible personhoods available to them (so that subjects are free to choose only from a predetermined selective reservoir of identities); and, on the other hand, how subjects can be said to be freely recreating new identities for themselves that are not already predetermined by power. In Patton's view, these two statements are not contradictory, and he argues that Foucault's concept of power has always presupposed the freedom of the subject in terms of the subject's capacity for action, despite the concept of freedom appearing late in Foucault's work:

> the power of an individual or body to act in certain ways is logically independent of relations to others and empirically the precondition of any action upon other bodies. In this sense, 'power to' [the capability to act] is conceptually prior to 'power over' [domination, or the exercise of power over others]. (Patton 1989: 270)

I contend that the philosophical concept of queer retains this sense of freedom as a 'power to', since the capacity for becoming other is based on a definition of the self as 'a relation of the human subject to itself in its power and its freedom' (SF 76). Everything hinges on this definition of the self – the possibility to critique authoritative discourses, the concept of queer, the sense of freedom, and thus the image of thought as well. Following Foucault, Halperin places an immense emphasis on this sense of the self as a 'strategic possibility' rather than a fixed identity (SF 76). But I would argue that the key to this understanding of the self lies in his definition of the self as 'a relation of reflexivity', for it is this sense that saves Halperin from falling back on the liberal notion of the self. Halperin clearly states what he means by 'reflexivity', though he does not expand on it: 'the "self" referred to here . . . is nothing but the bare *reflexive pronoun*' (SF 76, my emphasis). The grammatical reference places an emphasis on the self's modality of action, which means that the self is defined primarily by its capacity to act upon itself (auto-affection) rather than know itself (self-consciousness). This point cannot be overemphasised, because it determines the role of freedom as the movement that constitutes the image of thought. Selfhood is not conditioned by the freedom to exercise self-reflection or contemplation, but rather by the freedom of the self to affect its self from within. If there is such a thing as a will to freedom, this will is modelled not after a willing consciousness that does not depend on a living body, but after a living matter that does not depend on consciousness, and I use 'living matter' here in the broadest sense possible: one that encompasses the whole of life – human and non-human, organic and inorganic.

Freedom, then, can be seen as the condition for both resistance and subjectivation, none of which can be said to be free independently of the other or to precede the other: subjectivation is a free process undertaken by free subjects of action (agents capable of auto-affection), and in the context of this study, Foucault's otherwise cryptic remark that 'freedom is the ontological condition of ethics' (E 284) does indeed make sense.[44] Nevertheless, subjectivation can be carried out only in an agonistic social environment or situation – because nothing exists outside power-relations, and least of all the subject who comes into being as an effect of power-relations occurring within them. Moreover, practices of self-fashioning, or concrete 'practices of freedom' (E 284), do not simply 'originate' from the consciousness of the subject. Foucault is clear on this point: 'these practices are nevertheless not something invented by the individual himself. They are models that he finds in his culture and are proposed, suggested, imposed upon him by his culture, his society, and his social group' (E 291). Consequently, in the concept of queer, ethical subjectivation is bound up with the political where it is expressed as resistance; thus, the political – the site where resistance takes place or is actualised – must itself be constituted as furnished with spaces of freedom (or points of resistance) that are in some sense independent of the ethical, or created alongside it in the form of the environment in which ethical practices are carried out.

But why argue that resistance is conditioned by the *same* sense of freedom that conditions subjectivation, as I insist? We should recall that this argument is an attempt to determine the plane that constitutes the internal conditions of thought that make the concept of queer thinkable. As I argued earlier, queer as a concept presupposes freedom as the movement that thought claims by right, and thus freedom is not a concept but the pre-philosophical that lies at the heart of thought. As such, freedom cannot receive any given, predetermined sense from either politics or ethics (for which freedom is a concept), because both are in fact connected internally in the concept, and both are conditioned by freedom in a way that renders the statement 'queer is resistance by becoming other than oneself' meaningful. If the political were to be defined by a pre-given sense of freedom, transcendence would have been reintroduced to the plane, and freedom would have become a concept confused with the plane (a universal).

But there are at least two ways to show that this is not the case: one with the aid of Patton, the other with the aid of Deleuze. As I indicated earlier, Patton disputes the argument regarding a supposed break between Foucault's earlier and later conceptions of power, and argues that power in the sense of 'power to' had always been the primary sense of the term in all of Foucault's work. He refers to Foucault's definition of power-relations in the first volume of *The History of Sexuality*, where Foucault explicitly says that 'power must be understood in the first instance as the multiplicity of force relations immanent in the sphere in which they operate and which constitute their own organization' (HV1 93). Power-relations, then, in their particular yet not fixed formations throughout history, are effects of a play of forces that constantly struggle with each other (which is why power-relations are inherently unstable), and consequently transform any given formation of power into a different one. Foucault's definition of power-relations as an effect of the play of forces, I would argue, is what makes the political both distinguished from the ethical *and* free in the same sense as the ethical; for, as Patton explains,

> the force in question should be understood as prior to any determinate modality of action, prior even to bodies themselves in so far as individual bodies may be regarded as complex arrangements of forces. The force in question here is no more than a capacity to act or be acted upon, a capacity to effect and be affected. (Patton 1989: 273–4)

Freedom, then, can only be said to be the property of the play of forces, not of power-relations nor of subjects, and therefore neither of resistance nor of subjectivation. Both the exercise of power and resistance to power, and both the imposition of identities via subjugation and the creation of subjectivity via subjectivation, are free in the same sense, because they are both the effect (or the expression) of one and the same process – the spontaneous play or the constant, dynamic struggle of forces, each of which is becoming a capacity to act on another force or to be acted upon by another force throughout history.

The free play of forces is the shared milieu of both politics and ethics, and it is that which conditions and determines their interrelation. This view correlates with Deleuze's account of the relation between ethics and politics in his book on Foucault (F 94–123). Queer becomes a thinkable concept only if it takes the freedom of the play of forces as its condition, for only then can it realise resistance by becoming other. Freedom is nothing but the power to act and be acted upon, and as such it is the pre-philosophical that constitutes thought: 'thought is freedom in relation to what one does, the motion by which one detaches oneself from it, establishes it as an object, and reflects on it as a problem', says Foucault (E 117). This capacity to freely 'detach oneself' in thought from habitual behaviours and meanings in order to pose them as a problem constitutes what, following Deleuze and Guattari, I identify here as the movement that thought claims by right; one that comes from a radical outside that nonetheless inheres in the concept as its condition of thinkability, namely, the free movement that defines the play of forces. Queer as a philosophical concept necessarily involves free thought – one that is capable of acting (on itself and on others) and being acted upon (by itself and by others), and is thus capable of grasping the conditions that determine the degree to which thought itself becomes active or reactive under given historical circumstances. Only then does the concept become a critical tool for queer thought, and only then does change become possible:

> A critique does not consist in saying that things aren't good the way they are. It consists in seeing on what type of assumptions, of familiar notions, of established, unexamined ways of thinking the accepted practices are based ... Thought does exist, both beyond and before systems and edifices of discourse ... Criticism consists in uncovering that thought and trying to change it: showing that things are not as obvious as people believe ... To do criticism is to make harder those acts which are now too easy. Understood in these terms, criticism (and radical criticism) is utterly indispensable for any transformation ... as soon as people begin to have trouble thinking things the way they have been thought, transformation becomes at the same time very urgent, very difficult, and entirely possible. (POW 456–7)

I think that Foucault's words neatly summarise the constructivist move I have attempted to draw here. In order to think how to overcome or change what is unbearable in the present – in Halperin's account it was the reality of the AIDS crisis and all that ensued – queer can be viewed as a philosophical concept that is constructed to reconnect the severed link between resistance (political action) and subjectivation (ethical practice) by making them 'meaningful', that is, by expressing them at one and the same time, or in one infinite movement – resistance-by-becoming-other. Queer's conditions of thinkability are laid out on a plane of immanence where thought is that which is free – not the subject, nor the power of institutions with their policies and laws. The freedom of thought is *vital* rather than political or ethical in nature; a thought that discovers the conditions of both political resistance and ethical subjectivation, and takes them both to be immanent to a radical outside – the field of forces and their dynamics of affection to which thought itself is immanent. Freedom belongs to thought not because it represents itself to itself as free, as if it were the reflection of some transcendent consciousness that resides outside life in a static universe of ideas; rather, freedom belongs to thought because thought is capable of folding in on itself, of turning back on itself, so that it could struggle with itself to escape what it currently is – all the actual ways by which it affects itself and is affected by others. By escaping what it currently is, thought becomes other to carve a different future out of the unbearable present.

In this sense, too, the conceptual persona of Saint Foucault, the Exemplary Saint, is the emblem of the Free Person. 'Conceptual personae carry out the movements that describe the author's plane of immanence, and they play a part in the very creation of the author's concepts' (WP 63), and the Exemplary Saint is the thinker who critically explores thought's power to affect itself and others and to be affected by itself and others. In his ascetic practices of freedom Saint Foucault actualises the dynamics of thought's power, and personifies (in the form of a perspective constructed on the plane) thought's power to introduce a critical interval – and I mean 'critical' in the sense of both critique and crisis – between action and reaction; an interval that attests to thought's power to resist by transforming itself from within, so that what is considered impossible becomes a real possibility to change the present.

What Can a Concept Do?

From the first chapter of this study, I have been arguing that Halperin's concept of queer is not only foreign to queer theory, but also constructed outside of it. Ironically, although Halperin's definition of queer is often cited by scholars working on queer theory, he consistently and openly expressed his dissatisfaction with the uncritical nature of queer theory and marked his distance from it. As we have seen earlier, queer theory had rapidly transformed into a normalised academic practice (SF 113; NOR), a non-subversive form of 'theory' that reinforces rather than undermines current structures of power, and that is denuded of its radical potential to creatively change and undo our habitual ways of thinking (HTD 44–7). For Halperin, Foucault offers a 'non-theory' (SF 122) and even an 'anti-theory' (HTD 45) of sexuality precisely because he succeeds in diverting the question of sexuality from simple definitions and established truths (that is, from attempts to create theories *of* sexuality) to a critical rethinking of the function of sexuality in past and present power regimes with their objectifying authoritative discourses (SF 120–1). From *Saint Foucault* to his monumental *How to be Gay* it seems that Halperin almost completely abandoned his concept of queer in favour of a line of inquiry that intensifies a concept of gay subjectivity, which marks his growing detachment from queer theory. Already in the 2003 essay, he argued that queer has become 'a generic badge of subversiveness, a more trendy version of "liberal"' (NOR 341), because, in its process of normalisation, queer theory emptied out queerness from the specificities of its content, namely, the actual lives of gays, lesbians, transgenders and other sexual identities. He asserted that 'queer theory proper is often abstracted from the quotidian realities of lesbian and gay male life' (NOR 343), and this abstraction ironically results, he argued later, in a ubiquitous denial of the difference and specificity of gay culture; a denial founded on a heedless embracing of anti-essentialism: 'as queer theory has become more institutionalized, the understandable reluctance to accept essentialist assumptions about lesbians and gay men has hardened into an automatic self-knowledgement [sic] or recognition of *any* cultural patterns or practices that might be distinctive to homosexuals' (HTB 63, original emphasis).[45] Consequently, 'queer' and 'gay' assume a much less contradictory relation here than in *Saint Foucault*. The primary distinction Halperin does reserve is between queer politics and gay politics, and even that only partially, since his insistence on the cultural specificity of gay male subjectivity is informed by an attempt 'to reclaim the culture of pre-Stonewall gay men by connecting it with such post-Stonewall developments as the queer and transgender movements' (HTB 64). To all intents and purposes, queer does not obtain here the conceptual force that my reading assigns it, but rather functions as either an inclusive umbrella term for all not gay-specific sexual identities or as a sign that operates under the double sense of both the homosexual and the non-standard (HTB 8, 15).

Halperin's return to gayness can nevertheless be considered as a continuation of *Saint Foucault*'s queer vision in a specific, non-exhaustive trajectory. Gayness is not defined here in terms of identity but rather as a cultural practice: 'gayness, then, is not a state or condition. It's a mode of perception, an attitude, an ethos: in short, it is a practice' (HTB 13), and the book's title, *How to be Gay*, attests to its overall ethical framework, which is concerned with actual practices of self-fashioning that have been shaping gay culture and subjectivity throughout history. Concisely, then, *How to be Gay* can be seen as a study of specific actualisations of queer ethics and praxis whose conceptual structure Halperin presented earlier in *Saint Foucault*, and therefore as a critical reaction against the dissolution of their potential for self-transformation and political action at the hands of queer theory. Halperin's more recent work on sex and love maintains the difference between gay and queer that underlies his earlier texts: while his study of sex is driven by the rationale of his work on gayness in *How to be Gay* (2016: 3), his argument for the 'queerness of love' explicitly returns to *Saint Foucault*'s concept of queer, which not only reaffirms the indeterminate and strange sense of queer (2019: 406, 418) but also insists upon queer love's irreducibility to sexuality (2019: 419).

With the construction of queer as a philosophical concept, my aim was to gauge the concept's power to resist habitual thinking and to engage in a critical evaluation of both past and present contexts. While understandable and sustainable in their own right, Halperin's objection to 'theory' and his withdrawal from the concept of queer do not foreclose queer's conceptual power which, in my view, he relinquished far too quickly. The evolutionary scheme of Halperin's main works presented above might point to a possible reason for his growing uninterest in the concept of queer: the restrictive sense of 'theory' as a disciplinary academic method of establishing truths, which he holds responsible for turning queer into a harmless qualifier. As long as theory is considered in the restrictive sense above, my construction of the concept of queer as philosophical rather than theoretical is completely in accord with his criticism of queer theory. However, such a distinction between theory and philosophy remains strictly formal, and – as Rodowick recently made amply clear in his *Elegy for Theory* – is entirely contingent upon the changing historical context of the rivalry between theory and philosophy. Moreover, although Halperin considers Foucault's genealogy of sexuality a 'non-theory', his restrictive sense of theory does not necessarily chime with Foucault's own view. While Halperin considers 'theory' an institutionalised form of academic practice that he finds complicit with and affirmative of given power structures, Foucault defines theory as a toolkit intended to study the specificity of mechanisms of power and to build 'strategic knowledge' that could endow struggles against power with a better understanding of their effects and possibilities for action (PK 145). In an exchange with Deleuze, both Foucault and Deleuze argue that theory is opposed to power by nature because it is itself a practice, 'a struggle to undermine and take power side by side with those who are fighting' (DI 208). A distinction between theory and non-theory, then, is not necessarily called for. Halperin himself can be said to be 'doing theory' when he analyses the homophobic logic of authoritative discourses, and knowingly does so strictly from within structures of power that he himself acknowledges the impossibility of transcending.

For Deleuze, there is no significant distinction between theory and philosophy. In his concluding remarks to *Cinema 2: The Time-Image*, Deleuze makes no difference between film theory and film philosophy, and defines theory in the same way that he and Guattari defined philosophy as the practice of creating concepts (TI 280). But even more importantly, my insistence on constructing queer as a philosophical concept almost thirty years after *Saint Foucault* is rooted in the inherently political nature of constructivism. Philosophy for Deleuze and Guattari does not represent the world but rather intervenes in the immediate present. Philosophy's involvement with the present, that is, with its immediate surroundings or milieu, is that which makes it utopian and political: 'the word utopia therefore designates *that conjunction of philosophy, or of the concept, with the present milieu* – political philosophy' (WP 100, original emphasis). This is why philosophy for Deleuze and Guattari is *geophilosophy*: thinking comes about on a plane of immanence that forms the milieu of concepts; the concept consists of zones or areas of neighbourhood that are formed between its components. Both the creation of concepts and the laying out of planes of immanence are expressed in actual, historical states of affairs that determine the distinctive forms of both plane and concept, of problems and solutions. For this reason, my reconstruction of queer as a philosophical concept began by investigating its then-present milieu, its functioning as a solution to an actual problem, both of which are expressed in states of affairs. But constructivism is political and utopian precisely because it is not historicism; the concept itself is an event that cannot be exhausted by its actualisation in historical states of affairs: 'what History grasps of the event is its effectuation in states of affairs, or in lived experience, but the event in its becoming, in its specific consistency, in its self-posing as a concept, escapes History' (WP 110). Constructivism is thinking the event in its becoming, in its ahistorical transformation, which is guided by chance and contingency – indeed, by the contingency of the event's geographical surroundings – rather than by fate or historical necessity:

Philosophically Queer: Constructing a Concept

> Geography is not confined to providing historical form with a substance and variable places. It is not merely physical and human but mental, like a landscape. Geography wrests history from the cult of necessity in order to stress the irreducibility of contingency. It wrests it from the cult of origins in order to affirm the power of a 'milieu'. (WP 96)

For geophilosophy, asking why queer appeared as a concept in the US rather than in AIDS-stricken South Africa is a moot question, as are all the consequent debates over the concept's usefulness in non-American territories.[46] They only lead back to the same historical narratives that find queer necessarily originating in the history of sexuality in the West, preceding (feminist, black, lesbian) struggles, the so-called infiltration of French thought into American universities et cetera. Such questions and historical accounts can only overlook what is singular about the queer concept and the event of AIDS in the US, for they confine it to fixed narrative structures and historical reasoning against which the concept and the event are judged. But since the concept expresses a virtual event, that is, the ahistorical potentiality that encompasses not just present but also past and future actualisations, it is never entirely *of* history because it subsumes its future in the form of a potential for change – that part of itself marking the transformation of the present into a different future. Geophilosophy is interested in the power of the concept and in the virtual event; it asks what the concept can do and how the event can be actualised (or played out) differently, which is why geophilosophy is interested in becoming – how can we become other than what we currently are? What are our potentialities in this time and place? How can we create a different, that is, a new future? To this political end concepts are created, and each time they are, it is contingency rather than historical necessity that determines how the absolute plane of immanence is connected to a relative social milieu. A critique of the present, therefore, becomes possible, because the milieu has been changed, rethought, negotiated and resisted from within, so that a new transformed milieu can appear out of the present one.

By turning to reconceptualise 'gay' in its specificity, Halperin proves to be well aware of how the creation of concepts works: they are invented and designed to change their surroundings by resisting their current form. And with a new concept of gay, Halperin discovers an entire ethics that can both evaluate actual practices and explore their potential:

> 'Gay' refers not just to something you *are*, but also to something you *do*. Which means that you don't have to be homosexual in order to do it . . . And if gayness is a practice, it is something you can do well or badly . . . your performance may be evaluated and criticized by other people, gay or straight . . . Whence the common notion that there's *a right way to be gay*. (HTB 13, original emphasis)

A new problem (how to be gay?) and a changed milieu now determine which concepts are created and for which purposes, and they give new form and content to an insight inspired by Foucault that Halperin had already presented in *Saint Foucault*: that what gay people do with their sexuality is much more threatening for the heterosexual social order than the homosexual act itself; and that these practices create new ways of life that shape both identities and communities. Halperin's turn to gayness does not mean that the concept of queer has been exhausted; on the contrary, its utopian vision as a 'horizon of possibility', as a critical engagement with the ethical practices that shape gay individuals and communities in America, continues to inform his work, wherein he both analyses and evaluates these practices of gay subjectivation and explores their potential.

My own 'return' to queer is not an attempt to revive it in any simple sense, but to create it anew out of what Halperin's work made possible. Halperin's work enabled me to construct a philosophical concept of queer as well as the plane of immanence and the conceptual persona that are created alongside it. But all three already constitute a deviation from Halperin's work, since the problem has changed: in the United States, AIDS no longer predominantly appears as an immediate death threat but as a chronic, mostly containable condition. With the normalisation of AIDS and the dissolution of its urgency as a crisis, the characteristic practices of queer resistance – ACT UP activism but also New Queer Cinema – faded away. We are no longer queer, because queer is of the past.[47] But it is precisely this past, what we no longer are, which Foucault found so fundamental for resisting the present: for the past reveals the contingent nature of our current ways of life. By creating concepts we create the means, according to Deleuze and Guattari, to resist the present, because concepts express events rather than states of affairs, becoming rather than being, what we can be rather than what we are. The AIDS crisis and the queer response to it are relevant to us today, I would argue, precisely because we do not live them in their urgency any more; but their effects on our current lives and all that they made possible to

Philosophically Queer: Constructing a Concept

think, criticise and change are far from being exhausted. Foucault's thought drove Halperin to create queer as a concept that, instead of affirming what sexuality is, asks what we can do with our sexuality, how sexual practices can engender new subjectivities, social relations and ways of living that are not already given in the present. Deleuze's form of critique enabled me in turn to recreate a concept of queer that rather asks what we can do *without* our sexuality: what new ways of thinking, ethical practice and political action (both undetermined and undeterminable by sexual politics) became visible and thinkable with the emergence of queer resistance to the AIDS crisis? And why is it even important to consider it today? These questions inform and guide the discussion in the next chapter.

Notes

1. From a historical perspective, my argument here does not do justice to the complexity of the LGBT civil rights struggles before and after the Stonewall Riots. As historian John D'Emilio argues, the riots were a 'catalytic event' encouraging and enabling gay and lesbian activists to ally themselves with other radical political movements of that period, which 'set themselves against not only the American government, but most forms of institutional authority' (D'Emilio 2002: 82). Gay Lib demands were met mostly due to these movements' conception of social change, which defined their political activity in terms of the reform of laws and public policies and establishing the community's own institutions. At this stage of the argument, my point is neither to reduce nor unify the problems, goals and strategies of the movements that had been formed in the aftermath of the riots, nor to argue that the problem of authority did not 'belong' to them, but rather to insist upon the new, specific nature of the emerging problem of authority, which drastically differs from the problems confronted by the Gay Liberation movements and their conception of social change and political efficacy. For elaborate, historical and theoretical accounts of the Gay Lib movements, their goals and rationale, as well as the divisions within them, see Altman 2012; D'Emilio 2002; Herman 1993; Stein 2012: 79–142; Wilson 1993.
2. See Epstein 1996: 49–50, 55. Interestingly, there is no mention of the term GRID in South African virologist Barry D. Schoub's *AIDS and HIV in Perspective* (1999), one of the most popular and elaborate books on the epidemic, written by a specialist for non-specialist readers. While some researchers insist that this term never functioned as an official label for the syndrome, Epstein provides references to the official use of the term in academic publications of clinical research

(Epstein 1996: 381 n.19). Historian Marc Stein argues that the problematic term GRID was replaced with the neutral term AIDS thanks to gay and lesbian activists who convinced public health authorities to do so. But in spite of that, and despite the causal agent of AIDS being isolated as early as 1986, and despite its being established that the disease was transmitted through unprotected sex and exposure to contaminated blood, 'most U.S. Americans continued to associate the epidemic with homosexuality' (Stein 2012: 144). The link between AIDS and homosexuality, specifically gay men's sexuality and lifestyle, was established by multiple discourses perhaps erringly and too hastily, says Douglas Crimp, but it nevertheless determined the activist response to the crisis: 'the idea of AIDS as a gay disease occasioned two interconnected conditions in the United States: that AIDS would be an epidemic of stigmatization rooted in homophobia and that the response to AIDS would depend in very large measure on the very gay movements [Randy] Shilts and [Larry] Kramer decry' (Crimp 2002: 60). For more on the ways AIDS shaped the public image of gay men, see Crimp 2002: 278–9. On the construction of AIDS as a gay disease by biomedical discourses, see Treichler 1999: 42–8; Seidman 1997: 171–2.

3. ACT UP is an acronym for the AIDS Coalition To Unleash Power, an AIDS activist movement that was founded in New York in 1987. ACT UP is Halperin's primary example of queer politics and activism.
4. Halperin opens this chapter by stating that the first volume of Foucault's *History* was the intellectual text that most influenced AIDS activists, and that part of his aim is to explain how Foucault's notion of power, as it is presented in *The History of Sexuality*, had been embraced willingly and positively by activists, despite the fact that liberal critics from the Left found it extremely impeding for the mobilisation of a successful political opposition (SF 16, 21–4).
5. In Ancient Greek, the word means training, exercise and practice, but it also has a general meaning – a mode of life, profession and art. This second sense of the word was emphasised in the work of Pierre Hadot, who argued that philosophy was a way of life for male citizens in Antiquity, comprised of both theoretical discourse (thought expressed either in speech or in writing) and spiritual exercises (*askēseis*), whose goal was to transform the practitioner's modes of seeing and thinking so that he could better his life and relieve himself from suffering. Foucault was influenced by Hadot's conception of spiritual exercises (and clearly Halperin is aware of that; see SF 75), although the latter had some reservations about Foucault's use of the term. See Hadot 1995; 2002.
6. Such practices in Antiquity ranged from intellectual exercises such as reading, listening and meditating, to more active exercises such

as self-mastery, accomplishment of duties and training for death. See Hadot 1995: 82–125; Foucault, HS 292–4, 306–7.
7. *Ēthos* (ἦθος) in Greek has several meanings: it primarily meant an accustomed place, an animal's habitat. It then also came to mean custom, usage, a person's disposition or character, and in general 'manners' when used in the plural.
8. 'What makes it [the care of the self] ethical for the Greeks is not that it is care for others. The care of the self is ethical in itself; but it implies complex relationships with others insofar as this *ēthos* of freedom is also a way of caring for others' (Foucault, E 287). See also Foucault, HS 36.
9. Deleuze and Foucault were famously in disagreement over the senses and value of the concepts of pleasure and desire, which each of them assigned an almost completely opposite meaning. This surprisingly bitter dispute, among other reasons, drove the two friends apart (Dosse 2010: 316–18). For a critical review of Deleuze and Foucault's differences over these concepts, see Grace 2009.
10. According to the Oxford English Dictionary, the term 'fistfucking' originated from a practice among homosexual men, and it literally means 'to insert one's hand or hand and forearm into the rectum or vagina of (a person) as a means of sexual stimulation'.
11. In the very year of his death, Foucault himself admitted that the link between the ethical practice of the care of the self and a new form of politics had still been underdeveloped in his work (E 294).
12. Foucault defined 'games of truth' as 'a set of rules by which truth is produced . . . it is a set of procedures that lead to a certain result, which, on the bases of its principles and rules of procedure, may be considered valid or invalid, winning or losing' (E 297).
13. Treichler (1999: 62–3) offers a compelling analysis of the efforts to deny the fact that women could actually be infected with the new 'gay plague'.
14. 'I have been driven by an *instinct of survival* to want to expose the political operations that have brought about such a phobic construction of Foucault in the first place' (SF 6, my emphasis).
15. 'My relation to [Foucault] is indirect and secondary . . . it is entirely mediated, imaginary, and – why bother to deny it? – hagiographical' (SF 6).
16. Specifically, he should not be confused with a sympathetic character taking part in a philosophical dialogue, which then sets the concepts of the author against those of other philosophies, represented by antipathetic characters. Conceptual personae can be either sympathetic or antipathetic, but both are immanent to the image of thought or to the philosophical 'ground' the author constructs: 'even when they are "antipathetic", they are so while belonging fully to the plane that

the philosopher in question lays out and to the concepts he creates' (WP 63).
17. 'The "point of view" is neither a concept nor a plane but that which "personalizes" the absolutely impersonal plane by circumscribing a relative position on that plane. The conceptual personae, in other words, constitutes the impersonal field as a "perspective" which then "activates", or "insists upon" the creation of concepts' (MacKenzie 2004: 35).
18. 'The story of [Foucault's] life makes it possible to interpret his work, as both a thinker and an activist, as a series of evolving responses and resistances to the "conditions of possibility" that governed his own *énoncés*' (SF 157).
19. On the canonisation of saints, see Cunningham 2005: 28–53.
20. Halperin resists producing the 'truth' about Foucault not only because 'revealing the truth' is futile against the lies of homophobia, as I discussed earlier, but, following Foucault, because of the problematic relation between truth and power: '"truth" confers power on those who can claim access to it: it licenses "experts" to describe and objectify people's lives . . . [and] to write without ever having to answer *to* the subject of their descriptions *for* the consequences of those descriptions, because their privileged access to truth enables their power to manifest entirely in the guise of a legitimate authority that has no need of further justification' (SF 185).
21. 'I consider the kind of critique I am undertaking here to be *necessary* . . . but I also acknowledge it to be *futile* as a political intervention, because those dirty tricksters . . . are also the ones whose social privileges most insulate them from feeling the force of my objections' (SF 138).
22. The editor of Foucault's 1982–83 lectures, Frédéric Gros, remarks: 'from the first lecture Foucault wants therefore to define his own place within a philosophical heritage, as if he was declaring that through these studies of *parrēsia* he was problematizing the status of his own speech and the definition of his role' (in Foucault, GSO 379).
23. 'The components are presented here as verbs, but this is not a rule. It is sufficient that there are variations' (WP 25).
24. 'Power relations are both intentional and nonsubjective . . . There is no power that is exercised without a series of aims and objectives. But this does not mean that it results from the choice or decision of an individual subject' (HV1 94–5).
25. 'Their [power-relations'] existence depends on a multiplicity of points of resistance . . . These points of resistance are present everywhere in the power network' (HV1 95).
26. 'Queer politics, if it is to remain queer, needs to be able to perform the function of emptying queerness of its referentiality or positivity, guarding against its tendency to concrete embodiment, and thereby

preserving queerness as a resistant relation rather than an oppositional substance' (SF 113).
27. For critiques of Foucault's underdeveloped concept of the other, see Cordner 2008; Oksala 2005: 193–207.
28. '[Gay identity], though deliberately proclaimed in an act of affirmation, is nonetheless rooted in the positive fact of homosexual object-choice' (SF 62). Following Halperin's differentiation between gay and queer (which also involves affirmation but of a different kind – not of the positive fact but of the position of resistance), we can say that understanding gay identity as a positive, recognisable and definable content is a conception shared by both the historical authoritative form of power before AIDS and the anti-authoritarian tactics of the Gay Liberation movements. A definable and recognisable gay identity enables authoritative discourses to dominate through objectification (homosexuals become objects of clinical, psychological and forensic knowledge); but in their struggles to liberate themselves from domination, Gay Lib activists reclaimed the very identity used to pathologise them, except this time in an affirmative rather than a negative manner. Foucault was critical of this sort of liberation-by-reversal (or turning the negative into the positive without questioning or undermining that which is being 'reversed' altogether), and Halperin follows Foucault's critique to distinguish and explain the difference between the queer model of resistance and the gay model of liberation; for in the age of AIDS, the tactics of Gay Lib are deemed ill-suited to deal with the new homophobic form of domination through objectification: 'in order to reverse the discourses of contemporary homophobia, it is not enough to attempt simply to reclaim and transvalue homosexuality. The most radical reversal of homophobic discourses consists not in asserting, with the Gay Liberation Front of 1968, that "gay is good" . . . but in assuming and empowering a marginal positionality' (SF 61). I expand on this point in the next section.
29. See also Foucault, SAP 217; HV1 92, 93; E 167–8, 291–2.
30. Foucault expresses this notion elsewhere as well; see E 292.
31. For a similar critique of Foucault's liberal critics, see Simons 1995: 59–67.
32. Foucault defined liberalism in a broad sense as an art of governance where 'freedom of behavior is entailed, called for, needed, and serves as a regulator, but it also has to be produced and organized' (BBP 65). To this end, liberalism forms 'liberogenic' devices that both produce freedom and effectively rob people of freedom, 'devices intended to produce freedom which potentially risk producing exactly the opposite' (BBP 69). It is worth mentioning that this text was published in France almost ten years after Halperin's publication of *Saint Foucault*.
33. For Foucault's discussion of gay liberation movements, see FL 217; E 282–3; GS.

34. In Foucault's view, institutions are not exclusive sites of power, but rather apparatuses of state through which power-relations also crystallise. See HV1 96–7.
35. Resistance, then, is also not opposed to power: 'like power, it [resistance] would have to organize, coagulate, and solidify itself. Like power, it would have to come from "underneath" and distribute itself strategically' (FL 224).
36. 'We still say that THE plane of immanence is, at the same time, that which must be thought and that which cannot be thought. It is the nonthought within thought' (WP 59).
37. 'It is presumed that everybody knows, independently of concepts, what is meant by self, thinking, and being. The pure self of "I think" thus appears to be a beginning only because it has referred all its presuppositions back to the empirical self' (DR 129).
38. It should be remembered that becoming-other here is the movement that the two points of view of the queer concept share but also duplicate: a position where exercised power is transformed from within itself into a point of resistance; and selfhood, defined as self-reflexion or a relation of self to its self, is transformed from within itself into a new self.
39. Foucault defines agonism as 'a relationship which is at the same time reciprocal incitation and struggle' (SAP 222).
40. In Plato, says Foucault, 'I take care of myself so that I can take care of others. I practice on myself what the Neo-Platonists call *katharsis* and I practice this art of the cathartic precisely so that I can become a political subject in the sense of someone who knows what politics is and as a result can govern' (HS 175).
41. Foucault argues that such a shift away from the Platonic model of the care of the self began in the first and second centuries CE, where instead of the care of the self being a 'relay' to politics and the care of others, the self now takes itself as the ultimate object of care: 'one takes care of the self for oneself, and this care finds its own reward in the care of the self. In the care of the self one is one's own object and end' (HS 177). See also E 260.
42. 'Foucault made it clear that he did not recommend reviving the classical form of social relations; he invoked it merely to dramatize the possibility of multiplying the forms of association beyond the small number that presently exists' (SF 82).
43. See, for example, Dews 1989: 40; Taylor 1984: 154.
44. This remark is cryptic in its original context because Foucault does not elaborate on the ontological aspect of freedom and seemingly contradicts himself later. He makes this remark in between addressing two different issues: right after he criticises the modern notion of liberation as a practice of freedom, and before he describes the practices of freedom in Ancient Greece and Rome. On the one hand,

this argument acquires a strong sense of generality – not only from its position between Foucault's words on modern and ancient practices of freedom, but mainly from its explicit association with ontology. On the other hand, a little later he argues that freedom has a very specific political sense in Ancient Greece, which is not at all ontological: it means not being a slave – neither to other people nor to one's desires and appetites (E 286).

45. See also HTB 77.
46. As Cindy Patton insists, 'although the problems faced by [PWAs] were in many ways universal, and although global activism was strongly influenced by that in the United States, it nevertheless operated in different geopolitical corridors and had different local meanings and effects' (2002: xviii–xix).
47. Muñoz makes the exactly opposite claim: 'queerness is not yet here. Queerness is an ideality. Put another way, we are not yet queer ... Queerness is a structuring and educated mode of desire that allows us to see and feel beyond the quagmire of the present' (2009: 1). While I side with his utopian vision of queer, I am critical of his Hegelian–Marxist framework for understanding queer's utopian function, and of the problematic attachment of queer to desire and sexuality. I discuss this point in the introduction here and in the next chapter.

3

Pozitive Bodies of Resistance

Relays of Theory and Practice

While philosophy is political and even utopian, it is not prescriptive. It is a practice in its own right – a means for the critique and transformation of the present – but it is also inevitably tied to non-philosophical practices, such as political activism and art. In an exchange that took place in 1972, Deleuze and Foucault discuss a new relation between theory (or philosophy for that matter) and practice that has transformed the role of the intellectual in our days. 'Theory does not express, translate, or apply a practice; it is a practice – but local and regional, as you [Deleuze] say: non-totalizing', Foucault states (DI 207). And Deleuze confirms:

> Yes, that's what theory is, exactly like a tool box . . . A theory has to be used, it has to work. And not just for itself. If there is no one to use it, starting with the theorist himself who, as soon as he uses it ceases to be a theorist, then a theory is worthless, or its time has not yet arrived. (DI 208)

The intellectual no longer writes theories on behalf of the oppressed or oblivious people, as Kant and Marx envisaged their role. The only thing an intellectual can do is to create

> a system of relays within an ensemble, within a multiplicity of bits and pieces both theoretical and practical. For us, the intellectual and the theorist have ceased to be a subject, a consciousness, that represents or is representative. And those involved in political struggle have ceased to be represented, whether by a party or a union that would in turn claim for itself the right to be their conscience. Who speaks and who acts? It's always a multiplicity, even in the person that speaks or acts. We are all groupuscles [*sic*]. There is no more representation. There is only action, the action of theory, the action of practice, in the relations of relays and networks. (DI 207, translation modified)

Deleuze's choice of the term 'relay' emphasises both the active, practical nature of the work of theory and its implementation within a larger set of reciprocal relations between practices, of which theory is but one type. Foucault's view of the nature of thought and criticism (cited in the previous chapter), together with Deleuze and Guattari's conception of philosophy as an inherently political practice of creating concepts, extend this earlier formulation of the relations between theory and practice. Just as in *What is Philosophy?* philosophy, science and art are considered three distinctive creative practices of thinking that may occasionally need one another to make progression in their own field, so are theory and (non-theoretical) practice distinctive activities that nevertheless maintain a reciprocal relationship for the same purpose:

> as soon as theory takes hold in its own domain, it encounters obstacles, walls, collisions, and these impediments create a need for the theory to be relayed by another kind of discourse ... Practice is an ensemble of relays from one theoretical point to another, and theory is a relay from one practice to another. No theory can be developed without encountering a wall, and a practice is needed to break through. (DI 206, translation modified)

In this study the concept of queer functions as a relay between practices and, I would argue, it can be considered to function this way in Halperin's *Saint Foucault* as well, since it is embedded in and hence developed within a network of non-theoretical practices: what Halperin calls 'queer praxis', or the political activism of ACT UP; and 'queer ethics' and 'homosexual spiritual exercises', or cultural and sexual practices such as sadomasochism, fistfucking and gay clone culture. The concept of queer does not simply refer to these practices, nor does it represent them; rather, it forms an intelligible reciprocal relation with and between them. Queer makes them meaningful for one another in the sense that it 'reveals' one practice to be potentially beneficial for the other:

> Through the invention of novel, intense, and scattered bodily pleasures, queer culture brings about a tactical reversal of the mechanisms of sexuality, making strategic use of power differentials, physical sensations, and sexual identity-categories in order to create a queer praxis that ultimately dispenses with 'sexuality' and destabilizes the very constitution of identity itself. (SF 96–7)

Importantly, though, Halperin, like Foucault before him, is wary of any idealisation of these practices or of prescribing definite courses of action (SF 100), since these practices are experiments in our own becomings, that is, in 'our futurity' (SF 106), whose outcomes and political effects cannot be predicted or pre-decided.

Ethical subjectivation and political resistance, then, enter a double becoming in the concept of queer – they form zones of neighbourhood and function as the components of the concept. But they are themselves *concepts* of these practices, which means that they have their own components: 'in any concept there are usually bits or components that come from other concepts, which corresponded to other problems and presupposed other planes' (WP 18). Philosophically speaking, to define 'queer praxis' and 'queer ethics' *as* practices, Halperin needs to link them by some means in order to move from the concept of queer to these concepts of queer practices, without reducing 'queer' to a simple qualifier: 'it is in this way that, on a determinable plane, we go from one concept to another by a kind of bridge' (WP 19). This 'bridge' is what enables Halperin to argue for the political import of ethical practices, which underscores his adoption of Foucault's critique of gay liberal politics in the age of AIDS. Put differently, in order to argue that 'political activism . . . is an experiment we perform on ourselves so as to discover our otherness to ourselves in the experience of our own futurity' (SF 106), rather than seeing it as a struggle to liberate a repressed nature via the reformation of laws, Halperin needs to show how Foucault's understanding of ethics informs and benefits his own (and Halperin's) conception of politics; this way, he can define politics as an ethical 'spiritual exercise' and even claim that this experimental exercise is that which defines for Foucault and for LGBTQ+ people today 'the transformative practice of queer politics' (SF 106). To this end, he must form a kind of bridge that relates the concept of queer to other practices – one that reflects the movement between politics and ethics within the concept and on the plane. I contend that the bridge Halperin sets up is Foucault's concept of pleasure, but that in doing so an unaccounted hidden presupposition seems to inform and problematise his concept of queer.

The Missing Body

For Halperin, the key to understanding 'what, specifically, might constitute a queer way of life' (SF 81) – or a queer ethos (in the Foucauldian sense discussed earlier) that functions as the positive, creative practice of constructing new social relationships and modes of being, and that resists the limited and delimiting selection that current power structures allow – is Foucault's differentiation between desire, a concept that has acquired institutional currency (through Lacan, for example) and is used by power mechanisms to assign subjects a unitary, recognisable sexual identity that enhances and maintains these mechanisms' hold over the subject's life;[1] and pleasure, a rather vague concept that refers to intense experiences that Foucault and Halperin consider potentially self-transformative: 'pleasure is desubjectivating, impersonal; it shatters identity, subjectivity, and dissolves the subject, however fleetingly, into the sensorial continuum of the body, into the unconscious dreaming of the mind' (SF 95).

Following Foucault, Halperin gives a detailed account of practices that produce intense sexual pleasure (rather than sexual desire), such as sadomasochism, gay clone culture and fistfucking. Common to all these practices is a certain effect that Foucault describes as the desexualisation of pleasure: an experience of bodily sensations of sexual pleasure unbound to the specific function of the genitals. Desexualising practices involve 'the eroticization of nongenital regions of the body, such as the nipples, the anus, the skin, and the entire surface of the body' (SF 88). The modern subject of sexuality rediscovers her body's capacity to produce and experience intense pleasure beyond and sometimes without involving the familiar erogenous zones (the sexual organs), the specificity of which is used to assign her sex, gender, and thus to determine the normal or abnormal nature of her sexual desire. So considered, desexualising practices are potentially inventive and self-transformative, because in the sexual encounters where they come about the coherence of sexuality, as an identifiable feature of the subject's desire, is disintegrated by an intense experience of pleasure that frustrates any attempt to use definitive categories (such as sex and gender) to assign the practitioner an identity. For this reason, queer political resistance is not defined as the means to liberate sexuality, but rather to subvert it: 'modern techniques of power make use of sexuality in order to attach to us a personal identity, defined in part by our sexual identity; by attaching that identity to us, they attach us to themselves' (SF 95). Such desexualising practices that intensify pleasure for its own sake can become 'a means of resistance to the discipline of sexuality, a form of counterdiscipline – in short, a technique of ascesis' (SF 97). They are carried out collectively and are linked to 'other expressions of subcultural developments' (SF 99) that comprise a whole way of life – a queer ethos, a mode of existence.

Halperin does not argue that these practices are radical in themselves, nor that they are the only self-transformative practices, sexual or otherwise, that are potentially of political value. While he refrains from any prescriptions for political action, he does define 'queer politics', a politics of resistance rather than liberation, in terms of the experimentation of individuals and groups with ethical practices that effect self-transformation and self-constitution, and concludes that 'in this sense, perhaps it is not too much to say that Foucault produced the non-theory of which ACT UP is the practice' (SF 122). This link, or 'bridge', between an actual form of activism and actual desexualising practices is founded on Foucault's concept of pleasure, whose primary value lies in its ability to decentre the subject and undermine the coherence of identity. Put differently, pleasure is that which enables us to move from the concept of queer (resistance by becoming-other) to the related concepts of (queer) ethical practice and (queer) praxis; it is the bridge that takes part in constructing the external consistency of queer, and it fulfils the correlative function of otherness as a component that participates in the construction of queer's endoconsistency.

But when pleasure is constructed as a bridge on the plane of immanence, Halperin unwittingly reintroduces a simple body/mind dualism that sits uneasily with both the concept of queer, the related concepts of queer practices, and the image of thought as freedom. This is especially evident when he discusses the desexualising practices through which the subject discovers her or his own body to be a vast sensory surface susceptible to an experience of pleasure that transcends his or her assigned sexuality, and thus encounters the body as a radical otherness. Through pleasure, subjectivity then dissolves into 'the sensorial continuum of the body, into the unconscious dreaming of the mind' (SF 95). Bodily pleasure and unconscious processes of the mind are said to be only one expression (or example) of the relation of self to its self, which is rather defined by the capacity of the self to transcend itself and to experience otherness from within. And yet it is from this concept of pleasure, in which a simple model of body/mind dualism is implied, that Halperin proceeds to argue for the political import of spiritual exercises as a means to cultivate the impersonal self in modernity, and to explain its difference from ancient spiritual exercises: 'it is no longer divinity but history ... that guarantees us an experience of the Other at the core of our own subjectivity and brings it about that any direct encounter with the self must also be a confrontation with the not-self' (SF 104). The subject's determination by history is revealed, then, in genealogical inquiries (such as Foucault's) that are themselves considered a form of spiritual exercise through which 'the self discovers its past as that which dwells within its present and thereby come to recognize in itself its own alterity to itself' (SF 105). Through genealogical inquiry concrete spaces of freedom – 'of radical possibility that existed virtually in the present' (SF 106) – are uncovered, as are new possibilities to create a subject that is different from what it currently is. The notion of pleasure, then, enables Halperin to link the conception of desexualising practices to a broader definition of spiritual exercises in their modern form, and thus to redefine political activism as spiritual exercise.

What is missing from Halperin's argumentation, though, is a *concept* of the body, and, for that matter, a concept of the mind as well. 'When the plane selects what is by right due to thought ... it relegates other determinations to the status of mere facts, characteristics of states of affairs, or lived contents', write Deleuze and Guattari (WP 51–2), and this is precisely what body and mind are unwittingly reduced to in Halperin's argument: a sensory fact, an unconscious reaction. Either the mind surrenders to bodily sensations, as in the case of desexualising practices, or the body inexplicably disappears in the operations of a reflective mind, as in the case of genealogical inquiry – in both cases, the mind/body relation remains obscured in the notion of pleasure. But is it possible to construct a concept of practice, political or ethical, that does not determine or imply the role of the acting bodies and/or minds, those which carry out the practice? Does the definition of selfhood as a 'relation of reflexivity' sufficiently cover the practical actions of both body and mind? And with the overemphasis on the role of the body in desexualising practices, does Halperin not risk confusing 'relation of reflexivity' (the power to affect and be affected, the relation of self to its self as other) with self-reflection (the relation of self to its self as one and the same, a self identical to itself)? Consequently, the notion of pleasure seems to reintroduce transcendence into the plane rather than form an immanent bridge: instead of establishing a relation between ethical practices and political practices that resonates with their double becoming in the concept of queer (the becoming-ethics of politics and the becoming-politics of ethics), the notion of pleasure rather relates them by metaphor or analogy, one that seems to collapse the political into the ethical. While the political import of pleasure-producing ethical practices may seem plausible, the ethical value of political activism is not equally evident, unless activism is explained by an ethical metaphor: political activism is *like* or *analogous* to the ethical work of self-fashioning, which itself remains completely transcendent in relation to activism. Thus, queer's external consistency is compromised, since ethics seems tantamount to a self-identical model that political action only resembles, imitates or represents by way of analogy.

In contrast to his detailed discussion of ethical practices and their political value, Halperin does not expand on why ACT UP, which he considers a prime example of queer politics, should be seen as adhering to his principal definition of spiritual exercise – an experiment we perform on ourselves in order to become other than what we are. In the absence of such discussion, and in view of the overemphasis on the (thin conception of) the body's role in ethical practices implied in the concept of pleasure and the consequent reduction of political action to a self-identical model of ethics, we also find ourselves back with a transcendent idea of freedom – a universal *to* which ethical thought and practice are immanent, and which political action can only represent by way of analogy or resemblance; as if thought is considered free only in the sense that it is capable of reflecting above and beyond its material, sensory bodily experience, rather than itself being determined by thought's power to affect and be affected.

Conversely, if the ethical and the political are to be free in one and the same sense, in one and the same infinite movement of thought, the notion of pleasure cannot be used to link the concept of queer as 'a horizon of possibility' – in which ethics and politics enter into a double becoming expressed in the statement that queer is resistance by becoming-other – with the concepts of queer praxis and queer ethics. Rather, to maintain the immanent relation between concepts on the plane, the notion of pleasure must be substituted by (or subjected to) precisely the concept that is missing from Halperin's account, namely, the body; for not only does the notion of pleasure imply a simple definition of the body (as a sensory surface) that obscures how critical reflection relates to material experience, but it also advocates inadvertently a model of ethical practice that is of a *sexual* nature, however desexualising such practice may aspire to be, and if only by virtue of the evident absence of an account of non-sexual ethical and political practices. After all, when Halperin argues that ACT UP is 'genuinely queer' (SF 63) as a movement because it is 'broadly oppositional' (SF 63), that is, not specifically orientated by the exclusive objectives of sexual politics, he finds it necessary to explain how (what he considers) a very 'unqueer' movement such as Queer Nation emerged out of ACT UP: 'it was precisely ACT UP's contamination of sexual with nonsexual politics, and its supposedly myopic focus on AIDS, that generated the felt need for a movement like Queer Nation in the first place' (SF 63).² In view of such an explicit characterisation of ACT UP, we cannot simply accept that the notion of pleasure is that which connects the concept of queer to both ethical practices and political practices; as much as it is intended to undo 'sexuality', pleasure is nonetheless considerably associated with sexuality, if only dialectically, by virtue of its definition as a process of desexualisation or the detachment of bodily pleasure from the genitals. This also means that we can know very little (if anything) about the nature of ACT UP's 'contamination of sexual with *nonsexual* politics', since Halperin is silent about these hybrid political practices that he considers a prime example of queer politics. In fact, should his understanding of ACT UP quoted above not lead us to at least entertain the idea that ACT UP, *as* a prime example of queer politics, is rather something different than just another form of sexual politics? And if so, is it not possible to assume that desexualisation should have engendered a much more radical effect, one that might result in a reconstituted body which is not defined primarily in *any* relation to sexuality, regardless of how malleably and broadly sexuality might be defined?

As long as ethical practices are associated in the notion of pleasure too closely with sexual practices, so is queer political activism in the age of AIDS associated too closely with sexual politics, and there is a very good reason to dispute this association: for there is a manifest and intensely felt *non-sexual* quality to ACT UP's activism, which transcends the boundaries of sexual politics. I would even argue that this non-sexual quality bears the movement's true revolutionary potential, one that I later ascribe to the art of New Queer Cinema as well. Queer praxis and ethics, as they were manifested by activist and artistic practices at the beginning of the age of AIDS, have rendered visible, intelligible, and indeed possible, new ways to think not only sexual, racial, generational and other differences, but also existential differences: a whole new mode of existence, a style of life, appears in the queer moment – very much present and alive and yet not acknowledged as such. Perhaps because it was too early to account for its revolutionary potential; perhaps AIDS had to go global and be normalised first (in the West); perhaps digital technology, cyberspace and the global economy had to evolve drastically in a relatively short period of time before we could think it; perhaps we had to get accustomed to the indeterminate character of sexuality and become indifferent to sexual radicalism before we could reconsider its promise of political efficacy.[3]

My only contention is that in our present, after queer has undergone a very short course of history, it is now possible to identify and account for a new mode of existence, a way of life which is still in the process of transforming our lives today, and whose emergence at the queer moment can reveal something of its radical potential. Concisely, the concept of queer, with its related concepts of political and ethical practices, will be shown here to be rendering visible and intelligible *virality* as a mode of existence. There may be far too many factors and historical complexities that need to be accounted for in order to explain why the appearance of this new mode of existence can only be thought of now. However, if we are to account for this change by means of a Foucauldian analysis of power-relations, I think it might prove useful to regard the queer response to AIDS rather as a symptom of the crisis of disciplinary societies than a reaction against them, and, accordingly, as that which testifies to the emergence of what Deleuze called 'control societies'.

In an interview with Antonio Negri that took place in 1990, in the heyday of ACT UP's activism and New Queer Cinema, Deleuze's description of the changes that had been taking place makes plausible such a supposition:

> We're definitely moving toward 'control' societies that are no longer exactly disciplinary. Foucault's often taken as the theorist of disciplinary societies and of their principal technology, *confinement* . . . But he was actually one of the first to say that we're moving away from disciplinary societies, we've already left them behind. We're moving toward control societies that no longer operate by confining people but through continuous control and instant communication. (N 174)

In control societies, techniques of domination are no longer satisfied with structuring sites of confinement wherein power can be exercised efficiently over the subject: 'in a control-based system, nothing's left alone for long' (N 175) – power strives to constantly infiltrate everything and everyone, and new kinds of technologies, machines and forms of communication are developed to enable power to expand its grasp. 'Each kind of society corresponds to a particular kind of machine', says Deleuze, and 'cybernetic machines and computers' are those which correspond to control societies (N 175). It is unsurprising, then, that one of the most immediate threats to control societies is virality in all its variations (biological, computational), for a virus, which can move freely and possibly unnoticed and corrupt anything with which it comes into contact, may destroy an entire network of control. Indeed, 'it's true that, even before control societies are fully in place, forms of delinquency or resistance (two different things) are also appearing. Computer piracy and viruses, for example, will replace strikes and what the nineteenth century called "sabotage" ("clogging" the machinery)' (N 175). And if virality is that which posed one of the greatest dangers to the emerging control societies in the 1990s – already a decade of living with a new deadly disease that spreads by a viral agent endowed with the ability to corrupt and manipulate the human genome, the code that constitutes the organisation of the human body – then maybe it seems plausible to argue that the queer response was guided by a utopian vision to think virality as a liveable mode of existence, and that it realised this vision in its practices of resistance. Such an argument requires, then, not only a critique of Halperin's use of the notion of pleasure, as I presented above, but also a construction of the missing concept of the body.

The Poz: A Joyful Body, without Pleasure or Desire

To approach the missing concept of the body, I first completely withdraw from the concepts of pleasure and desire. This might seem, at first glance, preposterous, if not politically dangerous, to those who work in the field of feminism, LGBTQ+ studies and queer theory, where these two concepts and their relation to the concept of the body have been utilised so productively. My reasons are both methodological and political: methodologically, my aim is to take seriously the question of what a concept such as queer can do beyond its determination by the context of sexuality and its relation to other identity categories. I contend that although the problem of sexuality determined the context in which queer appeared, it is not that which defines the concept's potential, no matter in how many sexual states of affairs or bodies it has been actualised or made meaningful. In this study, the construction of queer as a philosophical concept is an attempt to acknowledge both the actual milieu in which the concept appeared as a solution *and* its virtual milieu and intensive features. The concept of queer – its components, its plane, its conceptual persona – is not essentially sexual in any way. Sexuality – be it an identity category, a lived experience, a device of power, and so on – conditions nothing for the concept of queer. Sexuality is of value here inasmuch as it signals its own destruction by something else, by this non-sexual quality called 'virality'. This does not mean that I simply dismiss the invaluable work still being done in any discipline that investigates sexuality as a problem, nor does it mean that sexuality, sex, gender and identity are problems of the past. They are obviously not. My goal is only to challenge sexuality as a definitive, rigid limit of thought, and consequently to reflect critically about what we can do *without* our sexuality.

For this reason, I also refrain from using Deleuze and Guattari's concept of desire. Not so much for the same reasons that Foucault somewhat half-heartedly accepted it (and still opted for pleasure);[4] Deleuze's concept of desire may work well for rethinking sex, as some have already shown.[5] My worry, though, is that Deleuze's concept of desire may not prove to be as productive for those who are less invested in the field of Deleuze studies.[6] My choice of concepts is not a matter of whim; rather, concepts are constructed in relation to their milieu, and I think that the closer the concept of queer gets to the limits of its familiar surroundings, the further it may find itself from sexuality. Indeed, to ask what a concept such as queer can do is to ask how far it can go before it becomes something entirely different, on condition that we stay within an immanent plane and refrain from subjecting the concept to transcendent principles, axioms or presuppositions from another discipline. Ruffolo's *Post-Queer Politics* is a good example of a critique of queer theory carried out in a Deleuzian, immanent framework, since he identifies queer theory's internal limitations and aspires to transcend them in a constructive, creative way (although he does not do away with sexuality or desire altogether). Penney's *After Queer Theory* goes precisely in the opposite direction, since he judges queer from the safety of pre-existing Marxist and psychoanalytical discourses, and is more concerned about saving sexuality from the way it has been handled by queer theory than about an affirmative investigation of the relations between queer theory and other discourses.

Politically, the still dominant affinity of the concept of queer with pleasure and desire is not simply a critical dead end but an obstacle or a 'wall', as Deleuze put it, to be tackled or overcome affirmatively and creatively. As Deleuze and Guattari say, 'nothing positive is done, nothing at all, in the domains of either criticism or history, when we are content with to brandish ready-made old concepts like skeletons intended to intimidate any creation' (WP 83).

Pozitive Bodies of Resistance

Critical thinking requires new concepts to be created, or old concepts to be transformed, in relation to new problems, and in new environments. We cannot assume, for instance, that the queer response to the AIDS crisis roughly thirty-five years ago can simply be repeated or reapplied today in response to the globalisation and normalisation of AIDS, and for this reason it seems equally implausible to assume that the concept of queer can be reapplied in contemporary theoretical contexts without undergoing significant modifications and adjustments. We are not facing the same problems any more, and queer's bond to sexuality seems today rather weak and encumbering with regard to certain contemporary problems, such as the problem of AIDS in Africa. For this reason, my aim is to take the concept to its limit, to see what it can do. At the outset, this means constructing the missing concept of the body independently of the concepts of pleasure and desire.

As we recall, Halperin argues that queer political activism is an experiment we perform on ourselves; a spiritual exercise through which we can discover our own otherness to ourselves, and become other. But the Foucauldian selfhood, as I constructed it earlier in the concept of queer, is a relation of reflexivity, a 'thin conception of agency', as Patton put it: the power to affect and be affected by itself and others. This conception of selfhood can be seen to parallel Foucault's concept of power-relations, which are themselves nothing but a provisional, relatively stable determination or a 'cut' made within the all-encompassing 'field' of unequal forces which act on one another and react to one another. The real, for Deleuze, is nothing but quantities of forces. As Deleuze's work on Foucault shows, selfhood as relation of reflexivity appears when a fold is created within the field of forces, and forms an interiority (F 97–100).[7] For Deleuze, the self that appears in Foucault's ethical writings is a fold that creates the inside of the outside, the latter being the reality of forces. Put simply, selfhood is the interiorisation of power, or power – in the sense of a capacity to affect and be affected – that forms a self-regulating assemblage of forces by redoubling itself from within. Spiritual exercises, then, are precisely quasi-autonomous practices of self-regulation of an interiorised power.

Selfhood, then, is a body in a Deleuzian sense: 'what defines a body is this relation between dominant and dominated forces. Every relationship of forces constitutes a body – whether it is chemical, biological, social, or political. Any two forces, being unequal, constitute a body as soon as they enter into a relationship' (NP 40).

The body, then, is a composition of forces, and the 'embodied self' here is nothing but an 'invagination' of forces, as Deleuze put it. But how do bodies come to be qualitatively different from one another? In Buchanan's account of Deleuze's Nietzschean–Spinozan concept of the body, a body is defined by its power or a specific set of practical capabilities that are determined by the relation between the forces of which the body is composed. These capabilities constitute the body's affect, which receives a specific qualification only when it is realised in the relations a body forms with other bodies. Therefore, 'affect is the capacity to form relations, while relations are only realizable to the extent that they can be connected to an existing capacity to form them' (Buchanan 1997: 81). All relations are subject to qualification, Buchanan adds, otherwise no difference can be instituted between bodies. He uses Deleuze's term 'health' to explain how relations are qualified: 'health here means, concisely, the actual measurable capacity to form new relations, which can always be increased, and the concomitant determination of whether or not the newly formed relations between bodies lead to the formation of new compounds, or the decomposition of already existing ones' (Buchanan 1997: 82). This also means, as Hardt notes, that the body is not a fixed unit but 'a dynamic relationship whose internal structure and external limits are subject to change' (1993: 92), and that, as such, the key to evaluating a given body's affect is to account for the body's self-motivated becomings, the 'active acts' by which the body itself becomes the active cause of its transformation rather than a passive receptor of the actions of other bodies or forces.

Once we account for the body's becomings, it is possible to qualify its affect, as well as its becomings, in terms of health or illness: the more relations a body can endure with other bodies, the greater its power; the more it lends itself to the process of becoming and is able to create new compounds out of it, the healthier it is (Buchanan 1997: 87). What qualifies a given body's power is not its ability to satisfy desires, nor its susceptibility to pleasure, but rather the experience of joy and sadness:

> [Good and bad] are the senses of the variation of the power of acting: the decrease of this power (sadness) is bad; its increase (joy) is good. Objectively, then, everything that increases or enhances our power of acting is good, and that which diminishes or restrains it is bad; and we only know good and bad through the feeling of joy or sadness of which are conscious. (SPP 71)[8]

Pozitive Bodies of Resistance

The joyful body (rather than the desiring or pleasuring body) is that which is able to increase its power in its encounters with other bodies; that is, when the relations it forms with other bodies result in compounds and affects, rather than in the decomposition of existing relations that leaves nothing in their place. In Deleuze's reading of Spinoza, this model of the body also serves as a means for evaluating and differentiating between good and bad actions. As an example, he presents Spinoza's discussion of the act of beating:

> What is good is that this act (raising my arm, closing my fist, moving rapidly and forcefully) expresses a power of my body; it expresses what my body can do in a certain relation. What is bad in this act? The bad appears when the act is associated with the image of thing whose [constitutive] relation is decomposed by that very act (I kill someone by beating him). The same act would have been good if it had been associated with the image of a thing whose relation agreed with it (e.g., hammering iron). Which means that an act is bad whenever it directly decomposes a relation, whereas it is good whenever it directly compounds its relations with other relations ... But what matters is knowing whether the act is associated with the image of a thing *insofar as* that thing can compound with it, or, on the contrary, *insofar as* it is decomposed by it. (SPP 35–6)

Similarly, in another example that Deleuze reviews, the act of eating, which is a relation formed between the body and food, can be qualified either as nourishing (good, healthy) if it increases a body's power to act, or as poisoning (bad, unhealthy) if it decreases the body's power to act: 'in this sense, there is no *evil* (in itself), but there is that which is *bad* (for me)' (SPP 33). The good and the bad are always relative because they are determined by the respective results of an encounter between bodies, but they do not exist in themselves from the point of view of nature or God (SPP 36). The key to understanding whether an encounter has been good or bad for us is in the feeling of joy or sadness, which are nothing but passions (affections, or 'feeling affects'), or an impression left on our body by another body (an external cause), as opposed to affect that is created by and from within our body (internal cause). Nevertheless, both joy and sadness may aid us in acquiring a better understanding of our power, and therefore in developing practical ways to control and arrange our encounters with other bodies, because these passions are indicative of the relative quality (good or bad) of our encounters with other bodies; of the relations we form with other bodies, whose effects we experience but whose cause may be unknown to us.

The conceptual 'bridge' provided by Deleuze's model of the body now allows us to trace a new sense or variation of queer political and ethical practices: the active experimentation with the body's affections, which is intended to enhance the body's power by increasing its capacity to be affected, that is, by entering into as many relations as the body can endure with other bodies without completely decomposing its own constitutive relation. What makes these practices queer, however, is that the body they have in mind – the one pushed to its limits – is a newly discovered body; one that they aspire to affirm rather than negate; one that they attempt to live and render liveable rather than mourn. It is not the homosexual body, nor is it any other pre-given form of the human body (gendered, racialised, ethnic, et cetera). *It is a joyful body that does not yet exist as such, but needs to be thought and imagined as such, or conjured up into existence* – the HIV-positive body, or what I refer to here as 'the Poz', the now common term for a person diagnosed as a carrier of the HIV retrovirus.

The Poz is an effect of an encounter between the human organism and what virologists identified as the 'Human Immunodeficiency Virus' (HIV), that is, the viral agent causing the clinical condition – considered fatal at least until 1996 – known as AIDS. Importantly, though, the Poz is not the sick body of the human subject; rather, it is that which has to be thought as a mode of existence, or a way of life, in its own right and to its full power, which also means that it is neither good nor bad in itself. Had it been predetermined as evil, there would not have been much to be done in the face of such a deadly and cureless disease, and the outcome of the encounter between the human body and the viral body then becomes both necessary and inevitable. The fact that today AIDS is still without a cure and yet *is* a liveable condition attests to the success of the political struggle to make AIDS liveable rather than fatal.

What links queer thought to queer practices, I contend, is indeed fighting AIDS, but this battle is not only against homophobia, prejudice, violence and indifference; nor is it simply another manifestation of humanity's struggle with aggressive non-human forces; rather, it is also a fight *for* and *with* AIDS – an active attempt to transform given relations between bodies in a given environment so that life, in an otherwise fatally transformed body, becomes liveable. This also answers the question as to why the queer activism of ACT UP cannot be reduced to sexual politics.[9] The common term 'person/people with AIDS' (PWA) has been rightly enjoying a political significance, because it resists the more common determination of one as a patient (in the sense of 'sufferer') or a sick person. But in this study, this term does not go far enough, since it separates 'the person' from a supposed 'condition' that this person currently inhabits, as if that condition has not painfully mutated that person's being and existence. The Poz does not refer here to a person with AIDS, but to a newly composed body with its own powers to affect and be affected. We should at least entertain the idea that the Poz cannot even be said to be entirely human, since the HIV retrovirus is endowed with a biological mechanism that enables it to reproduce itself within the hosting body by integrating a DNA copy of its genes into the DNA of the host's cells. This procedure (known in biology as 'reverse transcription') suggests the eradication of the fundamental difference between the human host and the invasive parasite – the two become inextricably intertwined at the level of the genome.

The Poz, as a liveable body, did not exist as such in the early years of the AIDS crisis, but had to be imagined, summoned and, indeed, invented. At the time there were just ill bodies, which were particularly manifested as sick male homosexuals. From a geophilosophical perspective, the association of AIDS with homosexuality was no more coincidental than the encounter between the human organism and the retrovirus. This relation between AIDS and homosexuality was determined in the way it was not because of historical necessity, but rather because of the contingency of the milieu in which it materialised. From the perspective of our present time, then, the differences between 'Western AIDS' and 'African AIDS' are more than a difference of 'the dynamics of the epidemic in a particular population' (Schoub 1999: 24); they are also differences of milieu that determine the way people respond to and make sense of AIDS. This also means that the queer response to AIDS in the United States cannot simply and solely be seen as an attempt to undo the link between homosexuality and disease so as to restore the status quo, although it was eventually compelled – by sheer historical circumstances – to be partially actualised through such an attempt. The queer response was also an affirmative experiment with a new mode of living, an invention of a new body whose power was not determined nor fixed by any pre-given human determinations, such as sex, gender and race. The power of this body, that is, the Poz, implies a new mode of existence that perhaps only today can be called 'viral'; but as an affirmative power of life, virality had been already implicated in queer politics and ethics.

ACT UP

The AIDS Coalition To Unleash Power was founded in 1987 in New York City, and it quickly spread and founded about 300 more branches across the United States as well as some in Europe. ACT UP was one of the first political movements to incorporate audio-visual media art into its actions and demos, and many of its members were skilled photographers, artists, graphic designers, videographers and film directors. They incessantly documented their actions, demos and meetings, and also produced an impressive number of educational videos, TV programmes (particularly for community television) and video clips. One of ACT UP's most prominent affinity groups, DIVA TV (Damned Interfering Video Activists), was founded in 1989 to document 'public testimony, the media, and community activism to motivate the fight against AIDS' (cited from ACT UP/New York website). And generally, members of such art collectives considered art inseparable from political action, and unapologetically enlisted the arts in the struggle against AIDS. Reflecting back on the unique graphics that came to be associated with ACT UP, Douglas Crimp describes the various artworks of ACT UP's collectives as an activist art, and decisively states that 'what counts as activist art is its propaganda effect' (Crimp 1990: 15). The point of departure of such artists, he says, is AIDS activism:

> social conditions are viewed from the perspective of the movement working to change them. AIDS activist art is grounded in the accumulated knowledge and political analysis of the AIDS crisis produced collectively by the entire movement. The graphics not only reflect that knowledge, but actively contribute to its articulation as well. (Crimp 1990: 19–20)

Today, the ACT UP archives are housed in the New York City Public Library. Former ACT UP members Jim Hubbard and Sarah Schulman created the ACT UP Oral History Project, an online collection of interviews with surviving members of ACT UP/New York. In 2002 the Tribeca Film Festival in New York presented former DIVA TV member James Wentzy's *Fight Back, Fight AIDS* – the first documentary about ACT UP. In 2012 two more documentaries about ACT UP were released: Jim Hubbard's *United in Anger* and David France's *How to Survive a Plague*, which won the Official Selection category at Sundance, and was nominated for Best Documentary Feature at the Academy Awards. Directors Wentzy and Hubbard kindly provided me with complimentary copies of their films long before they were released in digital format (in fact, Wentzy's film was not formally released, and at the time he gave me a copy it was almost impossible to get a hold of it. Today it is available online on Vimeo.) The following discussion is a direct continuation of my argument about the utopian vision of queer practices and how they were informed by the urgency to imagine the possibility of living as Poz. The details of the movement's structure and actions were gathered from the documentaries mentioned above, archive footage I reviewed at the NYPL, and scholarly publications. However, it is not my intention to offer a comprehensive understanding of the movement, nor a historical, fact-based account or a conclusive study based on qualitative research methods; rather, my argument is a philosophical and thus a speculative one. As such, it is selective in its discussion of materials, because my aim is not to argue that ACT UP activists intentionally concentrated their efforts on realising the Poz as a liveable body, but rather to show why it is productive to consider their actions and methods as indicating the possibility of a viral mode of existence, the imagining of which originates in an urgent necessity. The section on New Queer Cinema is guided by the same hypothesis.

Representations associating the deadly illness with homosexuality had not only been considered an effect of the AIDS crisis, but, in fact, its very foundation and a crucial problem for activism. Simon Watney writes:

> Now, more than ever, we need to understand clearly and precisely what forces and values are mobilising in relation to the ongoing crisis of AIDS. For AIDS is not only a medical crisis on an unparalleled scale, it involves a crisis of representation itself, a crisis over the entire framing of knowledge about the human body and its capacities for sexual pleasure. (Watney 1997: 9)

To make the Poz a thinkable and liveable body, ACT UP launched an attack against none other than the sick body, particularly against the sick homosexual or gay male body that had become the primary representation of the sick body. Activists invested a considerable amount of effort in fighting representations of sick, dying bodies, and many of the affinity groups of which the movement was comprised functioned to constitute what Saalfield and Navarro called 'counter-media', which created and put into circulation images of

PWAs as activists, fighters and heroes. Such were the images created by their fellow ACT UP member Lola Flash: 'PWAs are not victims. PWAs are only patients when they are hospitalized. And in Flash's photographs, AIDS activists – HIV+ or not – are presented as AIDS warriors' (Saalfield and Navarro 1991: 344).

But the function of ACT UP's counter-media does not come down to replacing negative representations with positive ones; rather, I would argue that in order to create the Poz as liveable body, ACT UP had to bring the system of representation itself into crisis. Following Deleuze, Dorothea Olkowski defines representation as 'the hierarchical ordering of categories that produces an objectified state of affairs' (1999: 14), that is, a static structure of homogeneous, quantifiable space and time. For Deleuze, the problem with representational thought – which constitutes the dogmatic image of modern thought – is that it presupposes transcendent criteria to determine meaning and essence: it judges phenomena and events according to predetermined conceptions of the real that supposedly lies beyond them, in an autonomous sphere of existence. In so doing, representation not only gives us a limited, static image of the world, reducing its richness and complexity to self-contained abstract ideas, but also forcefully subordinates difference and change to its universal view whereby they are treated as inessential, derivative variations of a pre-existent identity. As Olkowski notes, 'the system of representation, whether in the realm of philosophy, psychology, social and political theory, ethics, or aesthetics, operates by establishing a fixed standard as the norm or model' (1999: 2), against which people and their actions are judged to determine how successfully or poorly they adhere to the standard.

The standard model constitutes 'majority' as an abstract ideal, and minority as its deviant – that which fails to represent it:

> The difference between minorities and majorities isn't their size. A minority may be bigger than a majority. What defines the majority is a model you have to conform to ... A minority, on the other hand, has no model. It's a becoming, a process ... When a minority creates models for itself, it's because it wants to become a majority, and probably has to, to survive or prosper ... But its power comes from what it managed to create, which to some extent goes into the model, but doesn't depend on it. (N 173)

A minority, then, is not simply an identifiable, underprivileged social group, but is itself a variable potential for transforming the representational standard. To emphasise this point, Deleuze and Guattari make a further distinction between minority and becoming-minoritarian in *A Thousand Plateaus*. While 'minority' can be defined as a denumerable set of individuals constituting the smaller social group in relation to a ruling majority, 'becoming-minoritarian' designates a mode or a process by which the standard, constitutive of both majority and minority, is destabilised from within and consequently undergoes transformation. As long as the standard in Western thought and culture is Man, that is, the white, adult, Western, heterosexual male, 'women, children, but also animals, plants, and molecules, are minoritarian' (TP 291), that is, potential agents of social change. Minorities, they note, are not revolutionary in themselves; rather, they embody the possibility of revolutionising the dominant organisational principles of a social structure. But to become revolutionary, 'even blacks ... must become-black. Even women must become-woman' (TP 291). Women, blacks, Jews, homosexuals and other minorities are standardised, derivative identities that are constructed *as* minorities by and in relation to Man *as* standard. As such, they occupy a marginalised position in the social hierarchy (even if demographically and statistically they might form the larger group).

The most immediate sense of practices of queer resistance can be found, then, in ACT UP's refusal to be yet another advocacy group of an oppressed minority, for this only means leaving the representational standard intact, and, at the same time, surrendering the movement's revolutionary energy to the very same state institutions against which it had been fighting. Aronowitz argues that the evolution of the once militant Gay Men's Health Crisis (GMHC) movement into an official extension of the US government during the early years of the AIDS crisis dramatises the stakes of representation that led to the founding of ACT UP:

> Having been formed initially to fight for state and private support for AIDS services for an alarmingly growing community of HIV-infected gay men, [GMHC] gradually, and somewhat reluctantly, became a health provider and its 'movement' character receded in favor of service delivery and public policy 'advocacy'. By the late 1980s GMHC had become an adjunct of state and local governments seeking to enhance its own legitimacy among the now considerable 'out of the closet' gay and lesbian community. (Aronowitz 1995: 367)

For ACT UP, says Aronowitz, the problem was that by forsaking its radicalism, GMHC was reinforcing and conforming to the official liberal economic policy that rationalised the uneven distribution of public goods on the basis of the private sector's interests. ACT UP refused, then, to accept that such a political rationale outweighed the urgent need to provide public health services for PWAs and allocate funding for AIDS research.

Undermining the system of representation also meant refusing to play 'the number game', as Aronowitz puts it; that is, challenging the liberal state model of representative democracy, whereby a majority acquires the right to rule and establish policies on behalf of all citizens by sheer electoral numbers. This explains why ACT UP was not primarily concerned with 'correcting' negative representations in the media, reforming the law, or increasing the number of its official representatives: 'the presence of openly gay public officials or civic leaders is inadequate to *represent* the needs of those associated with AIDS, especially under conditions where determined, and more to the point principled, opponents exercise equal or greater force' (Aronowitz 1995: 365). Instead of fighting for better representation of PWAs and homosexuals, ACT UP was creatively experimenting with forming the conditions for PWAs to speak for themselves. This also meant displacing the model of representative democracy in favour of a model of radical democracy (Aronowitz 1995: 377), to which the movement's decentralised organisation clearly attests. Formal agendas and appointed leaders and spokespersons were substituted with multi-functional, ever-changing affinity groups and committees, which formalised their own agendas and courses of action, and, at the same time, took part in the movement's general assembly.

The decentralised structure of ACT UP also testifies to the movement's deep understanding that effecting social change by way of challenging representation means thinking relations as constitutive of bodies rather than as derivative of their fixed identity. The 'body' of the movement was an ever-changing multiplicity of relations between individual bodies and their respective forces, and these also determined the movement's capacity to organise and change its relations with its surroundings. This is why Deleuze's concept of the body so aptly links queer political practices and ethical practices with queer thought: by thinking the body in terms of its power to be affected – that is, its capacity to form relations with other bodies, to become other, so as to enhance its control over itself and its environment and consequently persist to exist – we are also discovering the contingency and instability of our most fundamental perceptions of what constitutes our environment, which means that multiplying relations between bodies may transform the spatial-temporal relations constitutive of their environment.

Practices that effect what Olkowski calls the 'ruin of representation' can be considered immanent expressions of the logic of queer activism: an active attempt to undo the constitutive relations that ascribe a fixed identity to both infected bodies and their environment. By becoming members in multiple and ever-changing affinity groups, ACT UP activists had become other than who they were as individuals or members in other movements, and provisionally created what Deleuze called 'blocs of space-time' that enabled not only PWAs but also the Poz to become thinkable and visible as a mode of existence. The problem for AIDS activism, then, was not only the possible or actual exclusion of sexual and other minorities *from* space (be it discursive, cultural, legal, private, public), but rather the newly imposed 'homelessness' of PWAs. Many of the movement's actions and demos can be seen as local attempts to challenge and transform the constitutive spatial-temporal relations of their environment. For instance, in December 1989 ACT UP held one of its most controversial actions at St Patrick's Cathedral in New York. Protesting against Cardinal O'Connor's edicts denouncing safe sex, and his constant condemnation of PWAs and LGBT people in general, ACT UP activists teamed up with members of WHAM (Women's Health Action and Mobilization) to organise the 'Stop the Church' action – a massive demo both inside and outside the cathedral. Outside, over 4,500 people blocked the streets calling 'Stop the Church!' and 'Curb your dogma!', stormed barricades set up by the police, and staged a massive 'die-in', a tactic of playing dead in the streets performed by hundreds of activists. Inside, a smaller group infiltrated the cathedral under the guise of parishioners attending Sunday Mass, and interrupted the sermon with acts of civil disobedience: some chained themselves to pews, others shouted invectives at the cardinal, threw condoms in the air, and played dead by lying down in the aisles. The die-ins turned the church into an ungodly place; similarly, in the Ashes Action, activists and their allies spread the ashes of their loved ones who had died of AIDS over the White House lawn, and literally turned it into a graveyard.

For activists, queerness, then, was 'a function of the diverse spaces in which it aims to become explicit' (Berlant and Freeman 1992: 156), which means that queerness is not pre-given in any identity but is constantly negotiated, transformed, and comes into being through and alongside the undoing of the relations constitutive of space. This transformative state of queerness, indeed, of the queer body of the movement, is inseparable from its formalised expression in what Deleuze and Guattari call 'collective enunciation', an impersonal, subject-less utterance whose function is to express the relations between bodies (their 'state') as constitutive of the function of a given or a called-upon collectivity.[10] Together, the state of bodies and utterances form an assemblage:

> Utterances are not part of ideology, there is no ideology: utterances, no less than states of things, are components and cog-wheels in the assemblage ... The only unity derives from the fact that one and the same function ... is expressed of the utterance and the attribute of the state of body: an event which stretches out or contracts, a becoming in the infinitive ... In an indissoluble way an assemblage is both machine assemblage of effectuation and collective assemblage of enunciation. In enunciation, in the production of utterances, there is no subject, but always collective agents: and in what utterances speak of there are no objects but machinic states. They are like the variables of the function, which constantly interlace their values or their segments. (D 71)

The movement's famous slogan 'We're here! We're queer!' in all its variations did not simply function as a performative speech act that created and rendered visible an identifiable community of speakers making claim on a 'here'; rather, it conveyed to activists and to the public their own transformation in the process of becoming, here and now. Together with its graphics and video art, ACT UP's collective enunciation became part of the movement's aesthetics of political pedagogy (Berlant and Freeman 1992: 155). As Douglas Crimp put it, the graphics 'enunciate AIDS politics to and for all of us in the movement', and after negotiating its formulation in words and colours, 'when the final product is wheatpasted around the city, carried on protest placards, and worn on t-shirts, our politics, and our cohesion around those politics, became visible to us, and to those who will potentially join us' (Crimp 1990: 20). It is in this assemblage that the Poz appeared and reappeared as the body and the speech of each and every ACT UP member, regardless of his or her HIV status, sexuality, gender, race, colour, social class or ethnicity.

New Queer Cinema

'New Queer Cinema' (NQC) is the name given by film critic and scholar B. Ruby Rich to a collection of films that won several prizes in independent film festivals mainly in the US in the early 1990s, and drew broad critical attention from critics, film scholars and audiences. Despite the vast aesthetic and thematic differences between the films, said Rich, they all exhibited a common style: 'Call it "Homo Pomo": there are traces in all of them of appropriation and pastiche, irony, as well as a reworking of history with social constructionism very much in mind' (Rich 2013: 18). Among the movement's films, one may find the Sundance Festival hits *Paris is Burning* (Jennie Livingston, 1990), *Poison* (Todd Haynes, 1991) and *Swoon* (Tom Kalin, 1992); as well as Derek Jarman's *Edward II* (1991), Gus Van Sant's *My Own Private Idaho* (1991), Gregg Araki's *The Living End* (1992) and many more.

Rich's general description of NQC's characteristics has been rephrased and further elaborated by other film scholars, but largely remained along the same lines.[11] In general, studies of NQC agree on the following points: 1) the crucial function of the political-historical context of the movement's emergence, namely, the AIDS crisis of the 1980s and the unique form of queer AIDS activism engendered by it; 2), which could be seen as the expression of (1), the questioning of identity politics and the category of identity as a whole, which marks the gay/queer conceptual difference for both political activists and scholars; 3) in relation to the question of content, provocative and powerful cinematic representations of sexualised subjects, challenging normative and moral conceptions of sex, gender and sexuality; and 4), in relation to the question of form, the strategic subversion of traditional cinematic styles, conventions, genres and narrative structures.

Both scholars and artists see AIDS as the *raison d'être* of NQC. Todd Haynes, who was also a member of ACT UP and its video collective Gran Fury, insisted in different interviews that what identified NQC as a group was its response to the AIDS crisis, 'but with a great deal of stylistic independence and opposition to norms' (White 2013: 140).[12] 'AIDS is why there is New Queer Cinema, and it is what New Queer Cinema is about', argues Arroyo (1993: 92), for whom the presence of an explicit or implicit relation to the pandemic distinguishes the films that are 'new' and 'queer' from those that are not. In a similar vein, Niall Richardson argues that the films of NQC are united 'by an attempt to mobilize many of the political and theoretical aims of queer and AIDS activism' (2009: 49). But the representation of AIDS alone does not suffice to label a film an NQC film. Some NQC films do include straightforward representations of AIDS (most notably Gregg Araki's *The Living End*, whose two protagonists are HIV positive; Jennie Livingston's documentary *Paris is Burning*; and Laurie Lynd's short *RSVP*, whose absent protagonist died of AIDS). But there were films about AIDS that predated NQC that are not even considered to be its precursors (for example, Bill Sherwood's 1986 *Parting Glances*, or Norman Rene's 1989 *Longtime Companion*, considered by many to be the first commercially released film to deal with AIDS, and which Todd Haynes thought was in fact a heterosexual film);[13] and there have been 'AIDS movies' coinciding with or antedating NQC that are not considered part of the movement nor of its successors (most notably Jonathan Demme's 1993 *Philadelphia*, and even Todd Haynes's 1995 *Safe*).[14] Many NQC films do not exhibit any relation to AIDS whatsoever, and yet are considered prime examples of NQC filmmaking (for example, Tom Kalin's *Swoon*, Derek Jarman's *Edward II* and Christopher Münch's *The Hours and Times* – all of them are set in periods that predate the AIDS crisis).[15]

Arroyo refers to NQC as a cinema made by and for gay man, and thus as one that is concerned with representing gay male desire and identities. He finds AIDS to be a necessary interpretative context that explains the historically specific nature of the fluid, unstable gay desires and identities constructed in the films. Employing a Jamesonian framework, he argues that 'the political unconscious of all of these films . . . are attempts to grapple with the ways in which the pandemic has changed our lives. Their style and narrative structure, however different, are attempts to represent them' (Arroyo 1993: 93). AIDS, then, informs these films' unique, untraditional style, their bold representations of sexuality, their engagement with death and their dystopian vision. The films, however, are not only aesthetic expressions of a mourning gay culture, argues Arroyo, but also a political intervention by artistic means – a direct continuation of the activist struggle against AIDS – that should be read as 'militant gestures, a particular form of ACTing-UP, and thus utopian' (1993: 94).[16]

Pearl takes her cue from Arroyo and argues that 'New Queer Cinema *is* AIDS cinema' but in a broader sense (Pearl 2004: 23). AIDS here is more than an interpretative context; it is a political-aesthetic logic that accounts for the representation of the diverse forms of disruption caused by AIDS. As such, Pearl argues that it can be applied to a wider group of films, and she therefore places AIDS not only at the level of the films' 'political unconscious' but also at the level of representation itself: 'The lack of coherent narrative, or genre recognition ... in New Queer Cinema, is partly a representational, or "artistic", reaction to the nature of retroviral behaviour. In other words, representation mimics the "narrative" of the virus' (2004: 24). Since the HIV retrovirus operates by disrupting the body's sense of self – by 'deceiving' the body into believing that it is its own enemy while the virus is its 'friend' – NQC, argues Pearl, responded with themes, plots and styles that 'reproduce' the various expressions of this disruption. The films' representations of fluctuating identities and fluid sexualities, as well as their fragmented narrative structures and the unusual construction of time, are the effects of NQC's ways of representing (and in some cases undoing or fictionally resolving) the disruptions caused by AIDS (Pearl 2004: 25).

This representational/aesthetic tactic was introduced to NQC, argues Pearl, by AIDS activism, for, in its various forms of civil disobedience, 'ACT UP itself mimicked the disruptions and unrest brought about by the retroviral HIV' (2004: 25). What linked AIDS activism to NQC, in their mutual effort to repeat or 'perform' with a difference the disruptions caused by AIDS, was a shared necessity: overcoming the unrepresentable nature of the virus, as well as the proliferation of misrepresentations in the mainstream media and public discourse of both the virus and PWAs. The growing availability and affordability of video technology enabled AIDS activists not only to persistently document demonstrations and floor meetings, but also to found alternative AIDS media dedicated to challenging and replacing what they considered to be dangerously misleading representations of AIDS and of PWAs (Juhasz 1995: 3). Pearl explains the migration of AIDS video activism tactics to NQC by indicating initially that directors Tom Kalin and John Greyson were themselves ACT UP members who embarked on their artistic career as video activists.[17] Later she pinpoints the similarities in the efforts 'to interrogate, rewrite and reassign responsibility' which characterise both NQC and AIDS video activism (Pearl 2004: 29). Benshoff and Griffin suggest a stronger link between NQC and AIDS video activism, arguing that 'AIDS activist videos – with their reappropriation and pastiche of mainstream imagery, as well as their desire to shock and confront – might be thought of as the blueprint for New Queer Cinema' (Benshoff and Griffin 2006: 221). Much like ACT UP itself, AIDS video activism was a heterogeneous collective of artists comprised of ever-shifting affinity groups within the movement. It assigned a political function to art that, according to Benshoff and Griffin, aimed to achieve a threefold goal: the creation of a 'counter-memory' of the AIDS crisis by means of documentation; counter-surveillance of police conduct at demonstrations; and the education of both the public and actual and potential members of the movement (2006: 212). Consequently, aesthetic techniques and effects (such as reappropriation and pastiche mentioned above) became inherently political: 'what counts in activist art is its propaganda effect; stealing the procedures of other artists is part of the plan – if it works, we use it' (Crimp 1990: 15).

In this study, I suggest a different view of the relation between queer thought and practices – and, therefore, between ACT UP's queer practices and NQC's cinematic practices – which somewhat departs from their current conception in scholarship. The key concept that links queer thought and queer practices is the body as Deleuze defines it – a multiplicity of relations between forces that defines a given body's affect, or its capacity to form new relations with other bodies that enhance its own power to exist. Queer is an embodied self only in this sense – a body that resists by becoming other, that is, by exploring its own affect or power to transform itself into a different, powerful arrangement of forces. As such, the queer body engages in an incessant transformation of its environment as well, and while the concept of queer implies a way of thinking that creates the immanent conditions of the concept's thinkability, the concept of queer practices – or what can be referred to as 'queering'– is a product of thought in which the becoming-other of the queer body receives a determinable expression as such.

But queering, so my argument goes, is not an attempt to express the becoming of just *any* body, but rather an active attempt to change the constitutive arrangements of bodies and their environment so as to render thinkable, imaginable and liveable an impossible body – which I call here the Poz. The Poz will not become a liveable mode of existence so long as it is thought in terms of the constitutive relations of the sick gay body, a dying deviant body which is divested of a time and a space; a spectre of existence that has no foreseeable future, confined to a narrow present in which it subsists rather than exists, for it merely awaits its inevitable demise. In this sense, the Poz is an impossible body, a body denuded of its power to exist; and queering is the utopian practice dedicated to summoning or inventing this body as a liveable one, a possible mode of existence. This utopian vision is the function that defines the relation between queer thought and queer praxis, and it therefore defines in this study what is 'queer' about the activism of ACT UP (its actions and demos, its organisational structure, its aesthetics, its enunciations) as well as the (no less political) artistic practices of NQC.

Consequently, with regard to ACT UP, I argue that the films of NQC are equally unconcerned with the system of representation, and are principally resistant to any simple attempt to integrate them into a unified, coherent phenomenon. As long as we remain within the constraints of representational thinking, the relations between NQC and ACT UP's activism, as well as the relations between individual films, may only seem suggestive, local and partial. For instance, if NQC is indeed AIDS cinema, it is unclear in what sense some NQC films (such as *Swoon*, *My Own Private Idaho* and *The Hours and Times*) address the AIDS crisis, other than by way of suggesting weak or strong analogies with the operations of the HIV virus, or simply by arguing that they had been created at the peak of the AIDS crisis. At the same time, it remains unclear what makes these films 'queer' except for the sexual identity of their directors or characters. The singularity of NQC, or its difference as an artistic movement, is no less obscure. In retrospect, Ruby Rich herself expressed such doubt: 'New Queer Cinema was a term more successful for a moment than a movement' (2013: 131).

Similarly, representational analysis fails to account for the singularity of individual films. Scholarly analyses of *Poison* are cases in point: almost all of them begin by retracing the three stylistically different narratives that comprise the film, and consider them three coherent storylines. It is unarguable that the film consists of three different parts that correspond to three titles – Hero, Horror and Homo – which are nonetheless given only in the closing credits. But what is left unaccountable is the way these three narratives are dissected to fragments throughout the film, which, in forming the film as a 'whole', are nothing but a patchwork of bits and pieces. Except for indicating that the three storylines are scattered throughout the film, the question of what constitutes the film's composition as a patchwork is unaccounted for. Can the concept of narrative structure ultimately account for the logic of each 'story' and for the way all three relate to one another?[18]

Against representational readings, I suggest considering queer thought and queer practices as the interrelated parts of a single queer assemblage: a provisional arrangement of heterogeneous parts, whose function is defined not by who or what it represents but by what it makes thinkable and possible despite and against representation – the Poz as a mode of existence, a liveable body, a 'chronic' way of life. The Poz is not the PWA, a term designating an already given self-identical body that 'got entangled' in a critical and possibly deadly 'state' but that nonetheless retains its constitutive relations; rather, the Poz is what the PWA *could* become if its constitutive relations as a new joyful body were to be affirmed. The Poz, then, is never given in any representation or actual body; it is called upon, invented, imagined. The philosophical concept of queer makes the Poz thinkable, while queer practices work to undo or transform the constitutive relations of bodies that thwart its realisation as such. For this reason, the queer practices of ACT UP and NQC can never be reduced to their sexual features, nor can the Poz be thought in any form of pre-given identities (sexual and otherwise) precisely because it 'appears' as the transformation of their constitutive relations.

And if the Poz is that which is summoned and called upon, this does not mean that it is the subject who dreams and fantasises about bringing it into existence. Rather, the Poz is summoned by a collective will, and is nothing but the utopian vision of this collective in its urgency to become other; indeed, to become a people that does not yet exist – what the sick gays are not yet, what PWAs are not yet – so as to escape what is unbearable and impossible in the present and to create the conditions for a different future. Therefore, the Poz, as that which a people-not-yet-in-existence wills, cannot be represented; rather, it is that which propels the becoming-minoritarian of ACT UP, and, in the same vein, that which makes NQC what Deleuze called 'political modern cinema', which the literature often dubs 'minor cinema'. When asked about the by now familiar labelling of his breakthrough film *Poison* as an NQC film, almost twenty years after winning the Grand Jury Prize at the Sundance Film Festival, Todd Haynes seemed reluctant to consider himself part of a strictly cinematic movement. It was more about 'what was going on in the streets than in the theaters', he said, and what his and other NQC films have in common is not simply an innovative cinematic style, but a commitment to a form of politics that is radically different from gay politics: 'The films that we're talking about here . . . had points of view that weren't just self-affirmations about being gay. They opened up whole ideas about strategies of resistance to homophobia, and how you depict the concept of "difference"' (qtd in Fear 2010: 69). Haynes expresses here an auteur position that could best be understood in terms of minor cinema, which is never about addressing predetermined subjectivities and communities, but instead about inventing new possibilities for their existence (TI 221–2; N 98).

NQC, then, did not set out to address or represent a community that was already out there – gays, lesbians, PWAs, blacks, Latinos – but to invoke a people, a future people, a possibility of living, a minority with no predetermined model: 'if there were a modern political cinema, it would be on this basis: the people no longer exist, or not yet ... *the people are missing*' (TI 216). NQC artists populate their films with characters and places caught in processes of becoming other than themselves, of experimenting with the elements that define them, of exploring new modes of thinking, talking and existing. That is why Deleuze argues that in minor or political cinema the people are missing – because they are no longer who they were, and they are not yet who they will be; they are in the process of becoming-other. We see this happening in *Paris is Burning*: it is not simply a documentary about the ball scene or the golden age of drag in New York City, but a fabrication of existence. Lives and events are recorded only in relation to this new way of being in the world. We get to know these people only by their new names, given to them once they were accepted into a 'house' – which is no ordinary house, but is loosely defined as 'a new meaning of family', 'a group of human beings in a mutual bond', or 'a gay street gang'. Members of a house are named after their houses, such as 'House of LaBeija', 'House of Ninja'. Every house is run by a 'mother', who is appointed by the members regardless of his or her gender, sex, age or ethnicity. Members talk about the founders of houses, of their legacies, of the houses' unique attributes. Everywhere we see peoples invented, negotiating their own rules and language. The film does not simply present us with a distinctive subculture, but with a dynamic, self-transformative collectivity and its practices of living.

The people are missing, says Deleuze, because they exist in a condition of minority – they are a multiplicity that shares a common problem or an impossibility that *must* be overcome, and for this reason they must come into existence. For this reason, all private concerns are inherently political; the private does not correlate to the political, but merges with it. In minor cinema, eliminating the boundary between the private and the political corresponds to new cinematic forms of fragmentation. Born out of social circumstances that made life impossible, collectivity in NQC films lacks a definite identity, and is expressed in the dynamic formation of groups that are in the process of negotiating their own rules of conduct. Unification by means of identity gives way to a fragmented existence that informs the aesthetics of the films. The style of NQC films is dictated by the lived experience of fragmentation, which is political through and through. The auteurs of NQC experimented with traditional styles, genres and narrative structures to reach the adequate compositional mode that is compatible with the fragmented experience of their characters. The logic of the films as a whole is a patchwork with no exclusive points of beginning or ending: *Poison* is constructed from images (scenes, narratives and styles) pieced together with no anchor points to guarantee the coherence of the film as a whole.[19] In *The Living End*, black screens randomly connect shots to produce an undetermined, circular space-time, much like the protagonists' journey, which has no end in itself other than to 'make place' for lives deemed impossible. Fragmentation, then, informs the creation of blocs of space-time: while abruptly cutting across places, times and events, the black screens (what Deleuze referred to as 'irrational cuts') actually reassemble a space-time of existence, which makes escaping violence possible. Music fulfils the same function in *RSVP*: coming from both within and without, from inside the diegetic space and form the overlaid soundtrack, it connects different places, people and the emotions they express. Music becomes what Deleuze considered a 'sound image' of an absent loved one who died of AIDS, but also of his omnipresence.

For Deleuze, minor works of art are not the products of gifted individuals, but of auteurs who can make their individual voice be heard only through a revolutionary, political demand: 'the author is in a situation of producing utterances which are already collective, which are like the seeds of a people to come, and whose political impact is immediate and inescapable' (TI 221–2). In Derek Jarman's *Edward II*, even speaking of personal death is made into a political utterance. In the closing scene, King Edward II's words in voice-over, talking of his death, express the birth of an untimely people seen in the image: a group of OutRage activists. Edward says: 'but of this I am assured. That death ends all, and I can die but once. Come death, and with thy finger close my eyes. Or if I live, let me forget myself.' While the fact of death remains final and private, occurring only once, life is realised only by dismantling the self, by self-forgetting; the 'I' surrenders to a collective, to an untimely togetherness visualised in the image.

Since the people are missing, they recreate blocs of space-time that can enable them to explore new modes of existence, or what they can become. When Julianne Pidduck looks back on the films of NQC, their unique historical moment of emergence during the AIDS crisis, and their relations with other films and artistic practices, to understand how they are relevant to the present day, she takes her cue from a question posed by the narrator in Mike Hoolbloom's short experimental video *Letters from Home*: 'We already know how we're going to die ... what we don't know ... is how we're going to live?' (Pidduck 2004: 86). In a sense, this could be said to be the question posed by each and every NQC film. But for Pidduck the 'broader question' becomes 'How should we represent AIDS now?' rather than what possible modes of existence *with* AIDS these films made thinkable and visible. Just as this question informed ACT UP's creative experimentation with the constitutive relations of space, it guided the creation of blocs of space-time in NQC films.

Let us take *Poison* as a case in point. The opening scene sets the tone for what seems like a recurring theme: the chase. We see policemen cornering Dr Tom Graves, the scientist who has managed to synthesise the human sex drive and has accidently drunk it in a moment of distraction. As Graves's body gradually deteriorates, society blames him for infecting people with a deadly disease that spreads sexual violence all over the city. When he feels as if his own home is closing in on him, he trashes it in frustration and looks up to an open window in the hope of escaping. Again and again we watch him literally running for his life, fleeing and being chased by the police, the mob and the people he has infected (including the woman he loves), and also by his own monstrous reflection. In a different time and place, but still in the same film, we hear the mockumentary testimonials of the people who knew Richie Beacon, the boy who shot his father and then miraculously flew out of the window and disappeared. We also meet John Broom, a young prisoner haunted by his desire for a fellow prisoner, Jack Bolton, and by memories of their past in a juvenile reformatory. Jack later attempts to escape prison and is shot dead. Different characters, different storylines, different cinematic designs – all are expressed in scattered images throughout the film, flowing in and out of each other, chasing each other's tail.

A comparison with a more recent film is especially useful for the analysis of NQC in this context, and for seeing the ramifications of imagining and imaging the Poz as a liveable mode of existence. Years after the height of the AIDS crisis, in Bruce LaBruce's film *Otto: or, Up with Dead People* (2008), this theme of escaping and chasing reappears in the story of a gay zombie named Otto, who is haunted by pieces of past life memories, and is chased and nailed down by zombie-bashers. Escaping but also chasing zombies reappear in the porno-political film 'Up with Dead People' (a film within the film) made by the fictitious director Medea, who choses Otto to be the protagonist of her film.

More than determining the characters' fate, all this chasing and escaping – this criss-crossing between diegetic and aesthetic thresholds – transforms the space they inhabit, as well as creating new relations between forces actualised in the image. These intensified movements of chasing and escaping, haunting and hunting down, persecution and resisting persecution, impelled AIDS activists to reclaim both the streets and art not simply as their 'own', but as a shared, collective site that transformed the constitutive relations of their environment; an imagined new space to live in. This newly transformed space emerges from the spectral quality of practices of chasing, escaping and resisting persecution. What haunts and is haunted is not the characters themselves; these merely trace out trajectories in an actualised space haunted by its own forces of becoming-other-than-itself, its virtual power. Rather, an unliveable space is substituted with one that *adds* dimensions to life by becoming other than itself. In its simplest form, this new space appears as superimposition: the placing of one image on top of another, which often makes one if not both appear semi-opaque, or acquire a quality of spectral transparency. For André Bazin, superimposition signals 'attention: unreal world, imaginary characters' (Bazin 2002). But in NQC, superimposition is but the elemental technique of adding more real to the image; of giving it more 'depth' by expressing new forces that challenge and transform anticipated and constitutive relations of space. As an expression of the transformation of space, superimposition not only refers to visible layers of an actualised diegetic space, but also to an impossible synthesised space that renders its processes of transformation (or its power) visible and thinkable.

In *Poison*'s last fifteen minutes we are presented with an unexpected image that contradicts and puts into crisis the entire mock TV documentary construction of 'Hero': the scene where Richie – only partly seen for the first time – kills his father and flies out of the window. The bedroom door, left slightly ajar, creates a threshold not only as a division of the diegetic space, but also between two stylistically different images and perspectives in one and the same image – a false division of space into two split worlds: that of

Pozitive Bodies of Resistance

Richie looking in, and that of his mother (in a Super 8 shot-within-shot) looking out, as if the two do not share the same space and time. Paraphrasing Fredric Jameson, what we see is how 'division relates': how the image is made inclusive by connecting Richie's supernatural world on one side of the door with the world of his bewildered mother. In sharp contrast to the realist, documentary-like, meticulous design of the images of interviews with the people in Richie's life (all of them constitute the 'after' of this event), this scene appears as the unmediated recording of a single event – THE event – that was not recorded and could not have been recorded (an event that constitutes the 'before' of the interviews' images). While the impossible recording of the event takes place before us in a 'now' that is nevertheless an impossible space-time for the 'Hero' images – because it has to be constituted as a 'before' that is in principle missing from the composition of retrospective interview images – the realism of the common-sense world recedes back to cinema and fiction by a double movement that is correlated to two different shots within the one shot (a different camera movement on each side of the door), and by the different 'tonality' or quality of the two worlds on either side of the door, effected by different film gauges. In this sense it can be said that two 'superimposed' spaces create the image of an impossible new space.

Superimposition becomes here more than a technical concept – it comes to express the transformation of relations constitutive of space. Once immanence was established in the image – the irrational linking of two different spaces in one impossible image – reality ceases to function as a criterion of differentiation between the true and the false, or the earthly (the documentable lives presented in interview images) and the supernatural (the fictionalised life of the boy who flew out of the window). Rather, cinema reveals its falsifying power to render thinkable and imaginable unrealised blocs of space-time. The flat face of the cinematic image reflects back a depth of space, a real added with dimensions: Richie's unearthly world that renders the testimonials about him contradictory and unrevealing. But this depth is also the image in excess, bearing within itself the interrelations between the two other series of images (or blocs of space-time) of Tom Graves ('Horror') and John Broom ('Homo'), along with their stories, their own haunted spaces and their unique styles. These three styles and their blocs of space-time are not metaphors for or analogies of one another, for they never appear to us as distinct whole entities; on the contrary, they coexist as the many moving parts of a fragmented whole that is the film itself – linked by montage and superimposed on one another to create a bottomless depth, wherein a plethora of real and virtual potentials for interrelations exceed by far their actualised counterparts. They constitute the film's artistic power, virtual series in which the logic of their fragmented temporal sequencing remains undecidable, thereby forming what Deleuze called 'lectosigns' – visual images that must be thought, deciphered and read as much as seen.

As with *Poison*, the queer 'technique' of superimposition continues to function as a sign of a synthesised space in LaBruce's *Otto*. With the character of Otto, every actualised space is doubled or superimposed at least twice: first seen through the zombie point of view in its unique auditions and visions, and second with past-living memories placed upon the undead's present in his aimless wanderings. But as a lectosign, it is also the image of the overlapping and interpenetration of LaBruce's film and Medea's film, each of them implied in one another: for what is Medea's politico-porno-zombie film 'Up with Dead People' if not LaBruce's own *Otto*, and vice versa? United in the title, neither film can be said to precede or be the cause of the other. Their relation remains undecidable, as symbolised by the scene where Medea shouts 'Cut!' and LaBruce cuts the shot of his own film. The question as to which one (*Otto* or 'Up with Dead People') is the film within the film is as undecidable as is Otto's existence as a zombie, or the reality of the terrifying 'gay plague' that infects the living and turns them into gay zombies; in the age of post-AIDS crisis, the plague is as literal as it is metaphorical.

The picnic scene is a prominent example of the queer superimposition technique, in which we see Medea, her brother Adolf and her girlfriend Hella having a picnic in a cemetery. Unlike the characters' openly stated doubts regarding Otto's ontological status as a zombie, no doubts are raised regarding Hella's mode of existence. Whenever we see her, Hella stands out as a character from the silent movie era; to be sure, not as an *imitation* of such a character, but as an actual image of a silent movie incorporated into the film's composition as a whole. She appears in black and white even if her surroundings are in colour; when she speaks, we see her lips move but a cheerful old tune is what we hear, followed by a slide repeating what she just said. Just like Otto, she is an image of an-other lived – and not imaginary – experience, and yet she does not seem to be confined by cinematic space-time and conventions. In the picnic scene, what we

Pozitive Bodies of Resistance

see is a dynamic coexistence of realities in a single space, two worlds in one: on the one side Medea's and Adolf's world of colour, and on the other Hella's world of black-and-white. The crossing-over between worlds appears entirely possible. As in *Poison*, the visible split screen is revealed to be inclusive rather than exclusive: Adolf is seen crossing in one continuous movement from the black-and-white side of Hella to the coloured side of Medea; Medea's hand crosses the visible split to serve Hella, who is in the other world, a cup of tea. When playing catch, the entire space turns black and white but without the silent movie tune, as if the two worlds have merged in a hybrid form. Colour cinematography becomes black-and-white cinematography without replacing or destroying it, but by superimposing two blocs of space-time that render visible and thinkable cinema's possibility of transforming itself through an image of its own past.

Similarly, when Medea announces the shooting of the final scene of 'Up with Dead People', the battle of the zombies against the living takes place on a giant bed, 'the final orgy of the dead' as it is referred to in the film. We see a group of raging zombie soldiers crossing over to the other side of the same room in one continuous movement, but on the other side they are naked and bloody and in black-and-white, and they embark upon an unmistakably real sexual act. A single space is now superimposed with forces of politics and pornography. Or, in Deleuzian terms, this new virtual space – defined by its internal difference, a divide effecting a false unity of space (irrational cut) – is the place where the becoming-pornography of politics and the becoming-politics of pornography occurs;[20] where a new expression of an alliance is created, one that had already been formed in AIDS activist videos and NQC.

Notes

1. 'I would say, schematically, that medicine and psychoanalysis have made extensive use of this notion of desire, precisely as a kind of instrument for establishing intelligibility of a sexual pleasure and thus for standardizing in terms of normality' (Foucault, GS 389); '[the notion of desire] is first and foremost attached to a subject. It's not an event; it's a type of permanent characteristic of the events of a subject' (GS 390).
2. For more on this problem, see Highleyman 2002: 107.
3. As Philip Derbyshire argued, 'yet it is one of the more extraordinary features of contemporary sexual culture that . . . erstwhile cutting-edge

sexual practices now find a strange normalcy, if not normalization – a sort of demotic popularization. The generalization of sexual deviance constitutes a severe blow to the *réclame* of sexual radicals' (2001: 26).
4. See Foucault GS 389–90.
5. See, for example, MacCormack 2008; Parisi 2004.
6. This has been the fate of Deleuze and Guattari's famous concept 'becoming-women' in feminism, which has not been received positively for a very long time. For discussions of this concept and its relations to feminism, see Braidotti 2002: 65–116; Buchanan 2000: 93–116; Grosz 1994: 160–83; Olkowski 1999: 32–58; Pisters 2003: 112–17.
7. For discussions of Deleuze's reading of the concept of the self as fold in Foucault, see Bogue 1994; Pelbart 2000; Stivale 2000: 6–7.
8. See also SPP 27–8.
9. Few recent studies make a similar claim, but they see the Poz as a then-new emerging identity rather than a body (see, for instance, Fung and McCaskell 2012: 192). I opt for the concept of the body because its Deleuzian model is more akin to the evaluation of capacities and processes of transformation – what the body can do and become – than to the identity which these processes effectuate.
10. For a discussion of collective assemblages of enunciation, see Bell 2018; for a detailed critical discussion of the concept of assemblage in Deleuze and Guattari's work, see Buchanan 2020.
11. See, for instance, Aaron 2004; Benshoff and Griffin 2006: 219–46; Richardson 2009: 47–80.
12. See also Wyatt and Haynes 1993: 7.
13. See Pettit 1991: 39.
14. See Pearl 2004: 32–3. Tom Kalin, director of *Swoon*, said in an interview that he actually considers *Safe* to be Haynes's queerest movie (Lim 2002: 43).
15. Despite the fact that *Swoon* was not about AIDS, Kalin said in an interview that he does consider the film a direct response to the AIDS crisis (Lim 2002: 43).
16. Similarly, Niall Richardson argues that 'Queer Cinema adopted the principles of ACT UP' (2009: 77). For Pidduck, that which is 'queer' about NQC 'derives centrally from an activist response to the AIDS crisis' (2004: 85).
17. As was Todd Haynes, who was a founding member of ACT UP's Gran Fury collective. See White 2013: 135.
18. For an analysis of *Poison* which is based on the reconstruction of three individual narratives, see, for example, DeAngelis 2004.
19. See Haynes's account of the strategies used in the editing of *Poison* (Leyda 2014: 40–1).
20. For an extended discussion on the relations between art, pornography and politics in LaBruce's films, see Brinkema 2006.

Conclusion: The Virality to Come, the Virality that Is

To say that the queer techniques and practices of ACT UP and NQC made it possible to think and imagine a viral mode of existence that was not yet in existence and yet urgently had to be imagined is to say that the Poz people who live among us today – with their practices of self-fashioning and aesthetics of existence – are, for better and for worse, the fruit of their creative political efforts. The Poz as such does not need to be wished for any more; it is already here, in many shapes and forms and in different communities across the globe. Some people today openly identify themselves as Poz, while for others there still is a Poz closet: they have their own magazines (such as poz.com), their own secret or open communities, and their own profile category in online dating apps. Tim Dean's *Unlimited Intimacy* argues that 'barebacking' has established a whole new subculture, and describes the emergence of a rich range of new meanings to describe Poz sex, such as 'barebacking', 'breeding' and 'seeding'; as well as new distinct Poz identities such as 'bug chaser' and 'gift giver' (Dean 2009). In July 2012 the US Food and Drug Administration approved the retroviral medication Truvada for use by HIV-negative people as preventative treatment (pre-exposure prophylaxis, commonly known as PrEP). 'Barebacking' was replaced with the somewhat less pathological and stigmatised term 'raw sex', and another transformation of the Poz sub-culture had begun, as raw sex entered the mainstream. Redistributing the terms used for denoting health and risk, freedom and resistance, this subculture opens up new ways to think, experience and make meaningful the Poz way of life (Dean 2015: 233–4, 241).[1]

These new Poz identities and practices have also been described as 'viral sex' (Blas 2012; Tomso 2008), post-crisis 'antiretroviral sex' (Florêncio 2020), 'viral ascetics' (Blas 2012) and as a means of biopolitical resistance (Tomso 2008). But if the Poz is already in the process of being shaped into identifiable subjectivities and practices, *virality* – as a mode of existence, a technology of control and of resistance, an arrangement of social and economic relations, or an affirmative technique of self-transformation – is still in the process of being realised, and its effects and potentials are far from being determined.² The queer assemblage created in the 1980s and the 1990s constitutes a past and a memory that informs the difference of our present, and that should all the more be explored as a rich source of possibilities for us to affirm and creatively transform our lives today.

Considering queer resistance in terms of Pozitive resistance, as this study insists, aims not simply to understand the past better, but rather, following Deleuze, to account for what we are in the process of becoming; the new form of society that is emerging. By reconstructing the queer concept and its immanent relation to the AIDS crisis as pure event, and by redefining queer practices of resistance as early manifestations of viral politics that target – and thus render sensible and conceivable – strategies of domination of emergent control societies, I am now able to relate the model of the Poz to contemporary modes of thinking, acting and living in a world that is becoming more and more viral. This study concludes that the body of the Poz can be used effectively to mobilise and address political, ethical and aesthetic theories and practices so as to unfold critically and creatively the dangers and potentials of a viral mode of existence in the present and the future.

I would argue that thinking virality as a mode of existence is an urgent task for the humanities today, particularly for theories and philosophies focused on questions of ethical practices, social change, responsibility and agency. Conceptualising queer in terms of Pozitive resistance can be used productively to trace out potential ways of rethinking and reimagining our freedom and its limits in today's control societies. It can be plugged into a growing body of interdisciplinary work so as to further explore and transform the infectious quality of viral, auto-affective processes of thinking and acting that are already shaping our cultural and political practices. Particularly, I find the concept of queer resistance in its Deleuzian formulation akin to and potentially useful for two contemporary discourses.

1) *Posthuman Thought*. Critically rethinking the decentring of the human by technological, informatic and economic networks, posthuman thinkers incorporate theories and methodologies from a vast array of disciplines to articulate the specificity of the human experience in our times, and to find adequate, practical means of thinking and acting in a world where the humanist tenets of anthropocentrism and speciesism no longer define the relation of human to non-human life forms. Posthuman thought requires a change of perspective that the model of the Poz can be seen to embody, for, as a composite

Conclusion

human–viral body, it is defined not as a diseased subject almost devoid of life, but rather as an *autopoietic* living entity – a metastable life-form capable of self-maintaining and self-reproducing. The model of the Poz is like a fractal, or a miniaturised replication of the emerging posthuman environment that we have come to inhabit; an interactive network society that is defined by a logic of contagion and that operates via 'an active principle of individuation, of assembling actors, which do not have to be constituted of humans but of various and varying agencies' (Parikka 2007: 294). ACT UP and NQC as early manifestations of Pozitive bodies of resistance attest to creative, imaginative ways of actively relating to immediate environments by effecting change *and* constantly undergoing self-transformation. As such, they amount to affirmative explorations of and experimentation with the viral mode of existence and its multiple forms of agency, in which selfhood and otherness are interconnected.[3]

2) *Parasitic Media Analysis*. A term coined by Finnish new media theorist Jussi Parikka, parasitic media analysis focuses on the status of objects or cultural products in the digital age, and thus can be considered the necessary counterpart of the posthuman challenge to subjective agency (Parikka 2007). Parikka offers to approach cultural objects as products of a viral logic of action ruled by symbiotic relations, and thus to turn analysis into a 'mapping tool' that can be used to navigate and explore the current phase of network capitalism. The aesthetics of queer resistance taps into the semi-autonomous lives of cultural autopoietic objects, and can redefine the ethical and political role of cinematic and new media arts today. For example, the online ACT UP Oral History Project reproduces the viral logic of the movement's tactics by creating a multilayered 'memory capsule', a digital archive that can be used to form an ethical relation between the founding generation of the movement and its heirs (Gill-Peterson 2013). The films of Bruce LaBruce, in another example, seem to take the queer aesthetics of resistance to extremes by experimenting with cinematic form and exploring the sexual lives of viral modes of being.

Notes

1. See also the recent collection of essays on the meanings and practices of raw sex, Varghese 2019.
2. See, for instance, Hui Kyong Chun 2011; Parikka 2007, 2013; Sampson 2012.
3. On posthuman thought, see, for example, Braidotti 2013; Wolfe 2010.

Bibliography

Aaron, M. (2004), 'New Queer Cinema: An Introduction', in M. Aaron (ed.), *New Queer Cinema: A Critical Reader*, 3–22, New Brunswick, NJ: Rutgers University Press.

Agamben, G. (2009), *What Is an Apparatus? And Other Essays*, trans. D. Kishik and S. Pedatella, Stanford, CA: Stanford University Press.

Altman, D. (2012), *Homosexual: Oppression & Liberation*, Brisbane: University of Queensland Press.

Aronowitz, S. (1995), 'Against the Liberal State: ACT-UP and the Emergence of Postmodern Politics', in L. Nicholson and S. Seidman (eds), *Social Postmodernism: Beyond Identity Politics*, 357–83, Cambridge: Cambridge University Press.

Arroyo, J. (1993), 'Death, Desire and Identity: The Political Unconscious of New Queer Cinema', in J. Bristow and A. R. Wilson (eds), *Activating Theory: Lesbian, Gay, Bisexual Politics*, 70–96, London: Lawrence & Wishart.

Bazin, A. (2002), 'The Life and Death of Superimposition (1946)', *Film-Philosophy*, 6(1), https://doi.org/10.3366/film.2002.0001.

Beckman, F. (2011), 'What is Sex? An Introduction to the Sexual Philosophy of Gilles Deleuze', in F. Beckman (ed), *Deleuze and Sex*, 1–29, Edinburgh: Edinburgh University Press.

Bell, J. A. (2018), 'Postulates of Linguistics', in H. Somers-Hall, J. A. Bell and J. Williams (eds), *A Thousand Plateaus and Philosophy*, 64–82, Edinburgh: Edinburgh University Press.

Benshoff, H., and S. Griffin (2006), *Queer Images: A History of Gay and Lesbian Film in America*, Lanham, MD: Rowman and Littlefield.

Berlant, L., and E. Freeman (1992), 'Queer Nationality', *boundary 2*, 19(1): 149–80.

Berlant, L., and M. Warner (1995), 'What Does Queer Theory Teach Us About X?', *PMLA*, 110(3): 343–9.

Blas, Z. (2012), 'Virus, Viral', *WSQ: Women's Studies Quarterly*, 40(1–2): 29–39.

Bogue, R. (1994), 'Foucault, Deleuze, and the Playful Fold of the Self', in R. Bogue and M. I. Spariosu (eds), *The Play of the Self*, 3–21, New York: SUNY Press.

Bibliography

Bordowitz, G. (2004), *The AIDS Crisis is Ridiculous and Other Writings, 1986–2003*, Cambridge, MA: MIT Press.
Braidotti, R. (2002), *Metamorphoses: Towards a Materialist Theory of Becoming*, Cambridge: Polity.
Braidotti, R. (2013), *The Posthuman*, Cambridge: Polity.
Brinkema, E. (2006), 'A Title Does Not Ask, but Demands That You Make a Choice: On the Otherwise Films of Bruce LaBruce', *Criticism*, 48(1): 95–126.
Buchanan, I. (1997), 'The Problem of the Body in Deleuze and Guattari, Or, What Can a Body Do?', *Body & Society*, 3(3): 73–91.
Buchanan, I. (2000), *Deleuzism: A Metacommentary*, Edinburgh: Edinburgh University Press.
Buchanan, I. (2020), *Assemblage Theory and Method*, London: Bloomsbury.
Butler, J. (1993), *Bodies That Matter: On the Discursive Limits of 'Sex'*, New York: Routledge.
Butler, J. (1997), 'Against Proper Objects', in E. Weed and N. Schor (eds), *Feminism Meets Queer Theory*, 1–30, Bloomington: Indiana University Press.
Butler, R. (2016), *Deleuze and Guattari's What is Philosophy*, London: Bloomsbury.
Carr, C. L. (2018), *Deleuze's Kantian Ethos: Critique as a Way of Life*, Edinburgh: Edinburgh University Press.
Conley, V. A. (2009), 'Thirty-Six Thousand Forms of Love: The Queering of Deleuze and Guattari', in C. Nigianni and M. Storr (eds), *Deleuze and Queer Theory*, 24–36, Edinburgh: Edinburgh University Press.
Cordner, C. (2008), 'Foucault, Ethical Self-Concern and the Other', *Philosophia*, 36(4): 593–609.
Crimp, D. (1990), *AIDS Demo Graphics*, Seattle, WA: Bay Press.
Crimp, D. (2002), *Melancholia and Moralism: Essays on AIDS and Queer Politics*, Cambridge, MA: MIT Press.
Cunningham, L. (2005), *A Brief History of Saints*, Oxford: Blackwell.
Dean, T. (2009), *Unlimited Intimacy: Reflections on the Subculture of Barebacking*, Chicago: University of Chicago Press.
Dean, T. (2015), 'Mediated Intimacies: Raw Sex, Truvada, and the Biopolitics of Chemoprophylaxis', *Sexualities*, 18(1–2): 224–46.
DeAngelis, M. (2004), 'The Characteristics of New Queer Filmmaking: Case Study – Todd Haynes', in M. Aaron (ed), *New Queer Cinema: A Critical Reader*, 41–52, Edinburgh: Edinburgh University Press.
Delehaye, H. (1962), *The Legends of the Saints*, trans. D. Attwater, New York: Fordham University Press.
D'Emilio, J. (2002), *The World Turned: Essays on Gay History, Politics, and Culture*, Durham, NC: Duke University Press.
Derbyshire, P. (2001), 'Homosexual Politics in the Wake of AIDS', *Radical Philosophy*, 109: 22–6.

Bibliography

Dews, P. (1989), 'The Return of the Subject in Late Foucault', *Radical Philosophy*, 51: 37–51.
Dosse, F. (2010), *Gilles Deleuze & Félix Guattari: Intersecting Lives*, trans. D. Glassman, New York: Columbia University Press.
Dowson, T. A. (2000), 'Why Queer Archaeology? An Introduction', *World Archaeology*, 32(2): 161–5.
Duggan, L. (2001), 'Making It Perfectly Queer', in A. Herrmann and A. J. Stewart (eds), *Theorizing Feminism: Parallel Trends in the Humanities and Social Sciences*, 215–31, Boulder, CO: Westview Press.
Edelman, L. (2004), *No Future: Queer Theory and the Death Drive*, Durham, NC: Duke University Press.
Eng, D. L. and J. K. Puar (2020), 'Introduction: Left of Queer', *Social Text*, 38(4): 1–24.
Epstein, S. (1996), *Impure Science: AIDS, Activism, and the Politics of Knowledge*, Berkeley: University of California Press.
Fear, D. (2010), '*Poison*'s Todd Haynes', *TimeOut New York*, 17(11): 69.
Ferguson, R. A. (2005), 'Of Our Normative Strivings: African American Studies and the Histories of Sexuality', *Social Text*, 23(3–4): 85–100.
Florêncio, J. (2020), 'Antiretroviral Time: Gay Sex, Pornography and Temporality "Post-Crisis"', *Somatechnics*, 10(2): 195–214.
Fung, R., and T. McCaskell (2012), 'Continental Drift: The Imaging of AIDS', *Queerly Canadian: An Introductory Reader in Sexuality Studies*, 191–95, Toronto: Canadian Scholars University Press.
Giffney, N. (2009), 'Introduction', in N. Giffney and M. O'Rourke (eds), *The Ashgate Research Companion to Queer Theory*, 1–13, Farnham: Ashgate.
Giffney, N. (2017), 'Introduction', in N. Giffney and E. Watson (eds), *Clinical Encounters in Sexuality: Psychoanalytic Practice and Queer Theory*, 19–48, Santa Barbara, CA: Punctum Books.
Gill-Peterson, J. (2013), 'Haunting the Queer Spaces of Aids: Remembering ACT UP/New York and an Ethics for an Endemic', *GLQ: A Journal of Lesbian and Gay Studies*, 19(3): 279–300.
Grace, W. (2009), 'Faux Amis: Foucault and Deleuze on Sexuality and Desire', *Critical Inquiry*, 36(1): 52–75.
Grosz, E. A. (1994), *Volatile Bodies: Toward a Corporeal Feminism*, Bloomington: Indiana University Press.
Grosz, E. A. (2010), 'The Practice of Feminist Theory', *differences*, 21(1): 94–108.
Hadot, P. (1995), *Philosophy as a Way of Life: Spiritual Exercises from Socrates to Foucault*, trans. M. Chase, Oxford: Blackwell.
Hadot, P. (2002), *What is Ancient Philosophy?*, trans. M. Chase, Cambridge, MA: Harvard University Press.
Hall, D. E. (2003), *Queer Theories*, New York: Palgrave Macmillan.

Bibliography

Halley, J., and A. Parker (eds) (2011), *After Sex? On Writing Since Queer Theory*, Durham, NC: Duke University Press.
Halperin, D. M. (2016), 'What is Sex For?', *Critical Inquiry*, 43: 1–31.
Halperin, D. M. (2019), 'Queer Love', *Critical Inquiry*, 45: 396–419.
Hardt, M. (1993), *Gilles Deleuze: An Apprenticeship in Philosophy*, Minneapolis: University of Minnesota Press.
Herman, D. (1993), 'The Politics of Law Reform: Lesbian and Gay Rights Struggles into the 1990s', in J. Bristow and A. R. Wilson (eds), *Activating Theory: Lesbian, Gay, Bisexual Politics*, 245–62, London: Lawrence and Wishart.
Highleyman, L. (2002), 'Radical Queers or Queer Radicals?', in B. Shepard and R. Hayduk (eds), *From ACT UP to the WTO: Urban Protest and Community Building in the Era of Globalization*, 106–20, London: Verso.
Hoad, N. (2007), 'Queer Theory Addiction', *South Atlantic Quarterly*, 106(3): 511–22.
Hughes, J. (2009), *Deleuze's Difference and Repetition*, London: Continuum.
Hughes, J. (2012), *Philosophy After Deleuze*, London: Bloomsbury.
Hui Kyong Chun, W. (2011), 'Crisis, Crisis, Crisis, or Sovereignty and Networks', *Theory, Culture & Society*, 28(6): 91–112.
Jagose, A. (1996), *Queer Theory: An Introduction*, New York: New York University Press.
Jagose, A. (2015), 'The Trouble with Antinormativity', *Differences*, 26(1): 26–47.
Jeffreys, S. (2003), *Unpacking Queer Politics*, London: Polity.
Juhasz, A. (1995), *AIDS TV: Identity, Community, and Alternative Video*, Durham, NC: Duke University Press.
Kedem, N. (2019), 'To Have Done with Sexuality: Schizoanalysis and the Problem of Queer-Feminist Alliances', in J. Sholtz and C. L. Carr (eds), *Deleuze and the Schizoanalysis of Feminism*, 111–26, London: Bloomsbury.
Keegan, C. M. (2020), 'Against Queer Theory', *TSQ: Transgender Studies Quarterly*, 7(3): 349–53.
Kemp, J. (2009), 'Schreber and the Penetrated Male', in C. Nigianni and M. Storr (eds), *Deleuze and Queer Theory*, 150–67, Edinburgh: Edinburgh University Press.
Kerslake, C. (2009), *Immanence and the Vertigo of Philosophy: From Kant to Deleuze*, Edinburgh: Edinburgh University Press.
Leyda, J. (ed.) (2014), *Todd Haynes: Interviews*, Jackson: University Press of Mississippi.
Lim, D. (2002), 'The Reckless Moment', *The Village Voice*, 19 March, 39–43.
Lundy, C., and D. Voss (eds) (2015), *At the Edges of Thought: Deleuze and Post-Kantian Philosophy*, Edinburgh: Edinburgh University Press.

Bibliography

MacCormack, P. (2008), *Cinesexuality*, Aldershot: Ashgate.

MacKenzie, I. (1997), 'Creativity as Criticism: The Philosophical Constructivism of Deleuze', *Radical Philosophy*, 86 (December): 7–18.

MacKenzie, I. (2004), *The Idea of Pure Critique*, London: Continuum.

May, T. (2005), *Gilles Deleuze*, Cambridge: Cambridge University Press.

McCann, H., and W. Monaghan (2020), *Queer Theory Now: From Foundations to Futures*, Basingstoke: Macmillan.

McKee, A. (1999), '"Resistance is Hopeless": Assimilating Queer Theory', *Social Semiotics*, 9(2): 235–49.

Mikdashi, M., and J. K. Puar (2016), 'Queer Theory and Permanent War', *GLQ: A Journal of Lesbian and Gay Studies*, 22(2): 215–22.

Muñoz, J. E. (2009), *Cruising Utopia: The Then and There of Queer Futurity*, New York: New York University Press.

Oksala, J. (2005), *Foucault on Freedom*, Cambridge: Cambridge University Press.

Olkowski, D. (1999), *Gilles Deleuze and the Ruin of Representation*, Berkeley: University of California Press.

O'Rourke, M. (2011), 'The Afterlives of Queer Theory', *Continent*, 1(2): 102–16.

Parikka, J. (2007), 'Contagion and Repetition: On the Viral Logic of Network Culture', *Ephemera: Theory & Politics in Organization*, 7(2): 287–308.

Parikka, J. (2013), 'Virality: Contagion Theory in the Age of Networks by Tony D. Sampson', *Theory, Culture & Society*, 30(3): 131–6.

Parisi, L. (2004), *Abstract Sex: Philosophy, Bio-Technology and the Mutations of Desire*, London: Continuum.

Patton, C. (2002), *Globalizing AIDS*, Minneapolis: University of Minnesota Press.

Patton, P. (1989), 'Taylor and Foucault on Power and Freedom', *Political Studies*, 37(2): 260–76.

Pearl, M. B. (2004), 'AIDS and New Queer Cinema', in M. Aaron (ed), *New Queer Cinema: A Critical Reader*, 23–35, New Brunswick, NJ: Rutgers University Press.

Pelbart, P. P. (2000), 'The Thought of the Outside, the Outside of Thought', *Angelaki*, 5(2): 201–9.

Penney, J. (2014), *After Queer Theory: The Limits of Sexual Politics*, London: Pluto.

Pettit, S. (1991), 'Reel to Real: A Conversation between Jennie Livingston and Todd Haynes', *Outweek*, 17 April, 35–41.

Phillips, K. R. (2002), 'Spaces of Invention: Dissension, Freedom, and Thought in Foucault', *Philosophy & Rhetoric*, 35(4): 328–44.

Pidduck, J. (2004), 'New Queer Cinema and Experimental Video', in M. Aaron (ed), *New Queer Cinema: A Critical Reader*, 80–97, New Brunswick, NJ: Rutgers University Press.

Bibliography

Pisters, P. (2003), *The Matrix of Visual Culture: Working with Deleuze in Film Theory*, Stanford, CA: Stanford University Press.

Rich, B. R. (2013), *New Queer Cinema: The Director's Cut*, Durham, NC: Duke University Press.

Richardson, N. (2009), *The Queer Cinema of Derek Jarman*, London: I. B. Tauris.

Rodowick, D. N. (2014), *Elegy for Theory*, Cambridge, MA: Harvard University Press.

Ruffolo, D. V. (2009), 'Post-Queer Considerations', in N. Giffney and M. O'Rourke (eds), *The Ashgate Research Companion to Queer Theory*, 379–94, New York: Routledge.

Ruffolo, D. V. (2016), *Post-Queer Politics*, London: Routledge.

Saalfield, C., and R. Navarro (1991), 'Shocking Pink Praxis: Race and Gender on the ACT UP Frontlines', in D. Fuss (ed.), *Inside/Out: Lesbian Theories, Gay Theories*, 341–69, New York: Routledge.

Sampson, T. D. (2012), *Virality: Contagion Theory in the Age of Networks*, Minneapolis: University of Minnesota Press.

Sartre, J.-P. (1963), *Saint Genet: Actor & Martyr*, trans. B. Frechtman, New York: Pantheon.

Schoub, B. D. (1999), *AIDS and HIV in Perspective: A Guide to Understanding the Virus and its Consequences*, 2nd edn, Cambridge: Cambridge University Press.

Sedgwick, E. K. (1994), *Tendencies*, Durham, NC: Duke University Press.

Seidman, S. (1995), 'Deconstructing Queer Theory', in L. Nicholson (ed.), *Social Postmodernism: Beyond Identity Politics*, 116–41, Cambridge: Cambridge University Press.

Seidman, S. (1997), *Difference Troubles: Queering Social Theory and Sexual Politics*, Cambridge: Cambridge University Press.

Simons, J. (1995), *Foucault & The Political*, London: Routledge.

Smith, D. W. (2012), *Essays on Deleuze*, Edinburgh: Edinburgh University Press.

Sontag, S. (1989), *AIDS and its Metaphors*, New York: Farrar, Straus and Giroux.

Stark, H. (2017), *Feminist Theory After Deleuze*, London: Bloomsbury.

Stein, M. (2012), *Rethinking the Gay and Lesbian Movement*, New York: Routledge.

Stivale, C. J. (2000), 'The Folds of Friendship – Derrida – Deleuze – Foucault', *Angelaki*, 5(2): 3–15.

Sullivan, N. (2003), *A Critical Introduction to Queer Theory*, New York: New York University Press.

Swarbrick, S. (2019), 'Nature's Queer Negativity: Between Barad and Deleuze', *Postmodern Culture*, 29(2), https://doi.org/10.1353/pmc.2019.0003.

Bibliography

Taylor, C. (1984), 'Foucault on Freedom and Truth', *Political Theory*, 12(2): 152–83.

Tomso, G. (2008), 'Viral Sex and the Politics of Life', *South Atlantic Quarterly*, 107(2): 265–85.

Treichler, P. A. (1999), *How to Have a Theory in an Epidemic: Cultural Chronicles of AIDS*, Durham, NC: Duke University Press.

Turner, W. B. (2000), *A Genealogy of Queer Theory*, Philadelphia, PA: Temple University Press.

Varghese, R. (ed) (2019), *Raw: PrEP, Pedagogy, and the Politics of Barebacking*, Regina, Sask.: University of Regina Press.

Wald, P. (2008), *Contagious: Cultures, Carriers, and the Outbreak Narrative*, Durham, NC: Duke University Press.

Warner, M. (1993), 'Introduction', in M. Warner (ed), *Fear of a Queer Planet*, Minneapolis: University of Minnesota Press.

Wasser, A. (2017), 'How Do We Recognise Problems?', *Deleuze Studies*, 11(1): 48–67.

Watney, S. (1997), *Policing Desire: Pornography, AIDS and the Media*, 3rd edn, Minneapolis: University of Minnesota Press.

Weiss, M. (2022), 'Queer Theory from Elsewhere and the Im/Proper Objects of Queer Anthropology', *Feminist Anthropology*, 3(2): 315–35.

White, R. (2013), *Todd Haynes*, Urbana: University of Illinois Press.

Wilson, A. R. (1993), 'Which Equality? Toleration, Difference or Respect', in J. Bristow and A. R. Wilson (eds), *Activating Theory: Lesbian, Gay, Bisexual Politics*, 171–89, Brisbane: University of Queensland Press.

Wolfe, C. (2010), *What is Posthumanism?*, Minneapolis: University of Minnesota Press.

Wyatt, J., and T. Haynes (1993), 'Cinematic/Sexual Transgression: An Interview with Todd Haynes', *Film Quarterly*, 46(3): 2–8.

Zourabichvili, F. (2012), *Deleuze: A Philosophy of the Event*, ed. G. Lambert and D. W. Smith, trans. K. Aarons, Edinburgh: Edinburgh University Press.

Index

A Thousand Plateaus (TP) (Deleuze & Guattari), 8, 127
ACT UP, 82, 100, 102n3, 114–15, 122, 124–30
   and New Queer Cinema (NQC), 133, 134, 135, 136, 147
admiration, 13–14
aesthetics of existence, 54–5, 83, 145
After Queer Theory (Penney), 24, 118
agonism, 87, 88, 106n39
AIDS, 36, 100, 115, 116, 122–3
AIDS activism, 4, 32, 33, 48–9; *see also* ACT UP; New Queer Cinema (NQC)
AIDS crisis, 51, 52, 119
   and activism, 48–9
   and concept of queer, 18–19, 20
   relevance today, 100–1
   and strategies of objectification, 58
Anti-Oedipus (AO) (Deleuze & Guattari), 2, 11–12
Archeology of Knowledge (AK) (Foucault), 138
Aronowitz, S., 127–8
Arroyo, J., 131, 132
askēsis / ascetics, 64, 71
   as spiritual exercise, 54
authority, 48, 51, 52, 62, 69–70, 79

Bazin, A., 140
'becoming-minoritarian', 127, 136
Benshoff, H., 133

Berlant, L., 34
biopower, 4, 5
body, 113, 114, 119–24, 125–6, 130, 134; *see also* Poz
body/mind dualism, 112, 113
Bordowitz, G., 19, 20, 33, 58
Buchanan, I., 11, 79, 120
Butler, J., 7, 22, 35–6, 38, 41, 42–3, 47n10

camp, 47n6
Cartesian *cogito*, 39–40, 44, 72–3, 84
cinema *see* New Queer Cinema (NQC)
Cinema 2 (TI) (Deleuze), 98, 136, 137, 138
closet, 50, 145
collective enunciation, 130
coming out, 50
communication, 44, 116
community, 30
concepts, 39–40; *see also* double-faced concept; gay (concept); queer (concept)
conceptual personae, 60–71, 95, 103–4n16
'Concern for Truth, The' (Foucault), 35
Conley, V., 23
constructivism, 9, 10, 37, 44, 45, 60, 62, 98–9
contemplation, 44, 91
control societies, 116–17, 146
creative ontology, 40–1

155

Index

Crimp, D., 19, 101–2n2, 124, 130, 134
critique, 41–2; *see also* Deleuzian critique; queer critique

Delehaye, H., 68
Deleuze, G., 1–3, 23, 118, 119, 126–7; *see also specific works by D.*
Deleuzian critique, 7–17, 48
  AIDS crisis, 52
  dual structure, 9–10
  genetic moment, 17
  pragmatic moment, 11–13
  problematic moment, 13–17
  queer's problem of definition, 32
  thinking queer, 27–8
delirium, 2
Derrida, J., 22, 23, 30
Descartes, R., 39–40, 44, 72, 84
Desert Islands and Other Texts 1953–1974 (DI) (Deleuze), 13–14, 98, 108–9
desexualisation,
  as ethical practice, 56, 59, 114–15
  as response to process of sexualization, 5–6
desexualising practices, 111–113
desire, 5, 56, 110–15, 118
Diabolical Saint, 65, 66, 71; *see also Saint Genet* (Sartre)
Dialogues II (D) (Deleuze), 3, 130
Difference and Repetition (DR) (Deleuze), 10, 12–13, 15, 16, 17, 18
dispositif, 3–4, 20n3, 56
DIVA TV, 124
dogmatism, 24, 41
domination, 52, 74–5, 82, 86–7, 90, 116, 146
double-faced concept, 72–9
Dowson, T., 22
Duggan, L., 22, 27

Edward II (Jarman), 131, 132, 138
ethics / ethical practice, 54–6, 75, 88, 89–90, 94; *see also* queer ethics; subjectivation
Ethics (E) (Foucault), 55, 69, 70, 74, 81, 87, 92
Exemplary Saint, 60–3, 72, 95
  v. Saint Genet (Diabolical Saint), 63–70, 71

false problems, 15–16, 32, 37, 40
feminism, 36, 38, 43
feminist theory, 33, 38, 41
film *see* New Queer Cinema (NQC)
Foucault Live (FL) (Foucault), 3, 5, 35
Foucault, M., 3–4, 5, 12, 40, 46, 75–6, 108, 109, 119; *see also Saint Foucault* (Halperin); *specific works by F.*
Free Person, 64, 71, 95
freedom, 43, 46, 64, 114
  and thought, 79–95

games of truth, 57, 103n12
gay (concept) / gayness, 99–100
  v. queer (concept), 84–5, 96–7, 105n28
gay identity, 105n28
gay liberation movements, 4, 52, 82, 101n1, 105n28, 110
Gay Men's Health Crisis (GMHC), 127–8
gay politics, 49–50, 54, 96; *see also* queer politics
'Gay Science, The' (GS) (Foucault), 1, 5
Genet, J. *see Saint Genet* (Sartre)
geophilosophy, 98–9
Giffney, N., 22, 23
government, 3, 75–6
Greyson, J., 133
Grosz, E., 38, 41

Index

Groupe d'information sur les prisons, 51–2
Guattari, F., 2, 14; *see also A Thousand Plateaus* (TP) (Deleuze & Guattari); *Anti-Oedipus* (AO) (Deleuze & Guattari); *What is Philosophy?* (Deleuze & Guattari)

Hall, D.E., 30–2
Halperin, D.M.
  concept of gay, 99–100
  concept of queer, 45–6, 48, 51–7, 59, 89: and authority, 60, 62; and Foucauldian concepts, 80–1; and freedom, 85–6; and queer theory, 95; relationship with queer praxis and queer ethics, 109–10, 114, 115–16; v. concept of gay, 84–5, 96–7, 105n28
  positionality, 35, 53, 76, 85
  queer activism, 119
  queer resistance, 87
  queer theory, 33–5, 41, 43, 53, 95–6
  see also specific works by H.
Hardt, M., 9, 120
Haynes, T., 131–2, 136
health, 120
Hermeneutics of the Subject, The (HS) (Foucault), 76–7, 89, 90
heterosexuality, 27, 32, 50–1
History of Sexuality, The (HV1) (Foucault), 3, 34, 50, 54, 58, 82, 93
HIV-positive body *see* Poz
homophobia, 49–50, 51
homosexuality, 27, 50–1, 55, 58, 123
How to be Gay (HTB) (Halperin), 96–7, 100
How to Do the History of Sexuality (HTD) (Halperin), 34, 95

Hubbard, J., 124, 125
Hughes, J., 7, 8

Idea, 44
immanence, plane of, 79–80, 84, 98
indifferentism, 41–2
intersubjective idealism, 44

Jagose, A., 21, 26, 28, 29
Jeffreys, S., 25
joyful body, 120–4

Kant, I., 16, 39–40, 41–2
Kemp, J., 23

Legends of Saints (Delehaye), 68
Letters and Other Texts (LOT) (Deleuze), 2, 12, 14
Letters from Home (Hoolbloom), 139
liberal thought, 81, 85, 90
liberalism, 105n32
Living End, The (Araki), 131, 132, 138

McKee, A., 53
MacKenzie, I., 37, 41–2, 44
majority, 126–7, 128
May, T., 40–1
Miller, J., 68
mind *see* body/mind dualism
minor cinema, 136–8
minority, 126–7; *see also* 'becoming-minoritarian'

Negotiations 1972–1990 (N) (Deleuze), 33, 40, 60, 89, 116–17, 126
Negri, A., 116
New Queer Cinema (NQC), 100, 130–43, 147
Nietzsche & Philosophy (NP) (Deleuze), 7, 9, 11, 119

Index

'Normalization of Queer Theory, The' (NOR) (Halperin), 33–4, 41, 95, 96
normative thinking, 22, 23

objectification, 56, 58, 59, 60, 87, 104n18
objective idealism, 44
objectivity, 44
Olkowski, D., 126, 129
ontology of discovery, 40
otherness, 55, 56, 71, 73, 76–9, 112, 119, 147
Otto: or, Up with Dead People (LaBruce), 139–40, 142

parasitic media analysis, 147
Parikka, J., 147
Paris is Burning (Livingstone), 131, 132, 137
Patton, P., 88, 90–1, 92–3, 119
Pearl, M.B., 132–3
Penney, J., 24–5, 118
'person/people with AIDS' (PWA), 122–3, 126, 128, 129, 133, 136; *see also* Poz
philosophy, 23, 37, 44, 45, 84, 98
  of difference, 40
  and practice, 108–10
  see also What is Philosophy? (WP) (Deleuze & Guattari)
Pidduck, J., 139
plane of immanence, 79–80, 84, 98
Platonic Idea, 44
pleasure, 5, 56–7, 110–15
Poison (Haynes), 131, 135, 136, 138, 139, 140–2
political activism, 110, 113–14; *see also* ACT UP; AIDS activism; New Queer Cinema (NQC); queer activism
politics, 75; *see also* gay politics; queer politics; sexual politics

Politics of Truth, The (POT) (Foucault), 76
post-Kantianism, 7, 17
Post-Queer Politics (Ruffolo), 118
posthuman thought, 146–7
power, 50, 51, 52, 81–2, 86–8, 90–1, 92–3; *see also* biopower
  and government, 3, 75–6
Power/Knowledge (PK) (Foucault), 97
Power (POW) (Foucault), 94
power-relations, 56–7, 77, 119
Poz, 122–4, 125–6, 129, 130, 133, 136, 145, 146–7
Pozitive resistance, 146
pragmatic moment, 11–13
pre-philosophical, 84
problematic moment, 13–17
problematisation, 13, 15, 16, 35, 69, 69–70
problems
  false, 15–16, 32, 37, 40
  true, 16

queer activism, 32, 119, 122–3; *see also* ACT UP; AIDS activism; gay liberation movements; New Queer Cinema (NQC); political activism
queer (concept), 17–20, 45–6, 48, 51–7, 59, 146
  abstractions of, 40–1, 42, 43–4
  and authority, 60, 62
  components of, 78
  as double-faced concept, 73–9
  and Foucauldian concepts, 80–1
  and freedom, 85–6, 88–9, 91, 93–5
  indeterminacy of, 21, 26–31, 37–9
  overdetermination of, 36
  as qualifier, 42
  relation between queer theory and, 34–5, 95

Index

relationship with queer praxis and queer ethics, 109–10, 114, 115–16
and resistance, 83, 87–8: and ethical practice, 89–90, 92, 94
and sexuality, 19, 117–18
v. gay (concept), 84–5, 96–7, 105n28
queer critique, 36
queer ethics, 109, 110, 112, 114, 115
Queer Nation, 114–15
queer politics, 41, 57, 76, 96, 110, 112; *see also* gay politics
queer practices, 110
and body/mind dualism, 112
of freedom, 70
philosophy as, 23
and queer thought, 122, 134, 135–6
sexual practices as, 56
see also queering
queer praxis, 109, 110, 112, 114, 115
queer resistance, 56–7, 83, 87–8, 100, 110, 146–7
and positionality, 35, 53, 76, 85
see also ACT UP; New Queer Cinema (NQC); queer activism; resistance
Queer Theories (Hall), 30
queer theory
and AIDS crisis, 18
criticisms, 53, 95–6, 118
'grounding axioms', 51
institutionalisation of, 19, 33–6
mis-introductions to, 26–32
paradox of, 21–5
as partial criticism, 42
sexuality in, 1, 4, 5–6, 22–3, 26, 31, 36, 42–3
Queer Theory Now (McCann), 32
queer thought, 6, 7, 17, 18

and queer practices, 122, 133, 135–6
queering, 6, 18, 22, 30, 42, 44, 53
of intellectual history, 31–2
of popular culture, 47n6
in queer theory, 34
see also queer practices
queerness, 129–30

reflection, 44
reflexivity, 91
resistance, 83, 85
and ethical practice, 89–90, 92
v. liberation, 49–50, 51, 54, 56, 112
and subjectivation, 94
see also political activism; queer resistance
Rich, B.R., 130–1, 135
Richardson, N., 131
RSVP (Lynd), 132, 138
Ruffolo, D.V., 24–5, 118

sadness, 120, 121
Saint Foucault (Halperin), 33, 45, 48–60, 85, 95–6
concept of queer, queer praxis and queer ethics, 109–11
desire v. pleasure, 110–15
Foucault as conceptual persona (Exemplary Saint), 60–3, 72: v. *Saint Genet* (Diabolical Saint) (Sartre), 64–70, 71
otherness, 77
power, 81–2
queer politics, 76
selfhood, 74, 91
sexual liberation movements, 82
Saint Genet (Sartre), 64, 65–7, 71
saints *see* Diabolical Saint; Exemplary Saint
Sartre, J.P., 64–7, 71
scepticism, 41
Schulman, S., 124

Index

Sedgwick, E.K., 50, 58–9
Seidman, S., 22
self *see* Cartesian *cogito*
self-fashioning / self-cultivation, 54–5, 76
selfhood, 74, 76, 77–8, 91, 119–20
sexual difference, 2, 38, 41
sexual politics, 43, 49, 82, 115, 122–3; *see also* gay politics
sexual practices, 56
sexuality, 50, 95–6
   in Deleuze, 1–3
   in Foucault, 3–4, 5
   overcoming of, 4–5 (*see also* desexualisation)
   and queer concept, 19, 117–18
   and queer resistance, 111
   in queer theory, 1, 4, 5–6, 22–3, 26, 31, 36, 42–3
   see also heterosexuality; homosexuality
sick bodies, 125–6, 134
signs, 12, 28
Smith, D., 39–40
Spinoza: Practical Philosophy (SPP) (Deleuze), 121–2
Stonewall Riots, 48, 101n1
'Stop the Church' action, 129
'Subject and Power, The' (SAP) (Foucault), 56, 71, 86
subjectivation, 64–5, 75–6, 78–9, 83, 86, 91–2, 94, 110
subjective idealism, 44
subjectivity, 74, 96, 112
Sullivan, N., 26–7, 28, 29–30, 47n6
superimposition, 140, 141–3

theory, 97–8
   and practice, 108–10
   see also feminist theory; queer theory
thinking / thought, 12, 16, 22–3, 27–8, 41, 79–95; *see also* posthuman thought; queer thought
time, 40
trans studies, 36
true problems, 16

Universal theorem, 43–4
universals, 41, 44
Unlimited Intimacy (Dean), 145
Unpacking Politics (Jeffreys), 25
US, 18, 21, 48–9, 100
utterances, 130, 138

value, 39
virality, 116–17, 118, 124, 145–6

Warner, M., 31, 34
Watney, S., 125
WHAM (Women's Health Action and Mobilization), 129
What is Philosophy? (WP) (Deleuze & Guattari)
   Cartesian *cogito*, 39, 73
   conceptual personae, 61, 62, 70, 71, 72, 95
   constructivism, 9, 10, 37, 98–9
   free thought, 85
   philosophy, 98
   plane of immanence, 79–80, 81, 83, 84
   universals, 44

EU representative:
Easy Access System Europe
Mustamäe tee 50, 10621 Tallinn, Estonia
Gpsr.requests@easproject.com

www.ingramcontent.com/pod-product-compliance
Lightning Source LLC
Chambersburg PA
CBHW070359240426
43671CB00013BA/2562